ENGLAND'S GLORY

Books by Vernon Coleman include:

The Medicine Men (1975)
Paper Doctors (1976)
Stress Control (1978)
The Home Pharmacy (1980)
Aspirin or Ambulance (1980)
Face Values (1981)
The Good Medicine Guide (1982)
Bodypower (1983)
Thomas Winsden's Cricketing Almanack (1983)
Diary of a Cricket Lover (1984)
Bodysense (1984)
Life Without Tranquillisers (1985)
The Story Of Medicine (1985, 1998)
Mindpower (1986)
Addicts and Addictions (1986)
Dr Vernon Coleman's Guide To Alternative Medicine (1988)
Stress Management Techniques (1988)
Know Yourself (1988)
The Health Scandal (1988)
The 20 Minute Health Check (1989)
Sex For Everyone (1989)
Mind Over Body (1989)
Eat Green Lose Weight (1990)
How To Overcome Toxic Stress (1990)
Why Animal Experiments Must Stop (1991)
The Drugs Myth (1992)
Complete Guide To Sex (1993)
How to Conquer Backache (1993)
How to Conquer Pain (1993)
Betrayal of Trust (1994)
Know Your Drugs (1994, 1997)
Food for Thought (1994, revised edition 2000)
The Traditional Home Doctor (1994)
People Watching (1995)
Relief from IBS (1995)
The Parent's Handbook (1995)
Men in Dresses (1996)
Power over Cancer (1996)
Crossdressing (1996)
How to Conquer Arthritis (1996)

High Blood Pressure (1996)
How To Stop Your Doctor Killing You (1996, revised edition 2003)
Fighting For Animals (1996)
Alice and Other Friends (1996)
Spiritpower (1997)
How To Publish Your Own Book (1999)
How To Relax and Overcome Stress (1999)
Animal Rights – Human Wrongs (1999)
Superbody (1999)
Complete Guide to Life (2000)
Strange But True (2000)
Daily Inspirations (2000)
Stomach Problems: Relief At Last (2001)
How To Overcome Guilt (2001)
How To Live Longer (2001)
Sex (2001)
We Love Cats (2002)
England Our England (2002)
Rogue Nation (2003)
People Push Bottles Up Peaceniks (2003)
The Cats' Own Annual (2003)
Confronting The Global Bully (2004)
Saving England (2004)
Why Everything Is Going To Get Worse Before It Gets Better (2004)
The Secret Lives of Cats (2004)
The Cat Basket (2005)
The Truth They Won't Tell You (And Don't Want You To Know) About The
EU (2005)
Living in a Fascist Country (2006)
How To Protect & Preserve Your Freedom, Identity & Privacy (2006)
The Cataholic's Handbook (2006)
Animal Experiments: Simple Truths (2006)
Coleman's Laws (2006)
Secrets of Paris (2007)
Cat Fables (2007)
Too Sexy To Print (2007)
Oil Apocalypse (2007)
Gordon is a Moron (2007)
The OFPIS File (2008)
Cat Tales (2008)
What Happens Next? (2009)
Moneypower (2009)
Bloodless Revolution (2009)

Catoons From Catland (2009)
101 Things I Have Learned (2010)

novels
The Village Cricket Tour (1990)
The Bilbury Chronicles (1992)
Bilbury Grange (1993)
Mrs Caldicot's Cabbage War (1993)
Bilbury Revels (1994)
Deadline (1994)
The Man Who Inherited a Golf Course (1995)
Bilbury Pie (1995)
Bilbury Country (1996)
Second Innings (1999)
Around the Wicket (2000)
It's Never Too Late (2001)
Paris In My Springtime (2002)
Mrs Caldicot's Knickerbocker Glory (2003)
Too Many Clubs And Not Enough Balls (2005)
Tunnel (1980, 2005)
Mr Henry Mulligan (2007)
Bilbury Village (2008)
Bilbury Pudding (2009)

as Edward Vernon
Practice Makes Perfect (1977)
Practise What You Preach (1978)
Getting Into Practice (1979)
Aphrodisiacs – An Owner's Manual (1983)

with Alice
Alice's Diary (1989)
Alice's Adventures (1992)

with Donna Antoinette Coleman
How To Conquer Health Problems Between Ages 50 & 120 (2003)
Health Secrets Doctors Share With Their Families (2005)
Animal Miscellany (2008)

ENGLAND'S GLORY

VERNON COLEMAN AND
DONNA ANTOINETTE COLEMAN

BLUE
BOOKS

Published by Blue Books, Publishing House, Trinity Place, Barnstaple, Devon
EX32 9HG, England.

ISBN: 978-1-899726-19-6

A catalogue record for this book is available from
the British Library.

Printed by CPI Antony Rowe

DEDICATION

Dedicated to everyone who is proud to be English and prepared to say so, to those who care, and to all those who have fought for England, whether at war or peace.

England Evermore

England's glory until the end
Our beautiful country we shall defend
From those who seek to destroy her name
We'll see England forever remain
We pledge to those who have fought before
Your time in battle we shan't ignore
So let's stand united in our quest to save
Let us be strong, let us be brave
England's glory until the end
Our beautiful country we shall defend.

By Donna Antoinette Coleman 2010

PREFACE

There is a widespread view among politicians and journalists that praising England, and the English, is racist. When the Scots or the Welsh talk proudly of their heritage that is regarded as a fine thing, to be applauded. But when the English do the same there are frowns and sneers. Schools in England teach children very little about England's proud history. Moreover, there is a strong tendency for commentators to credit all the great things our nation has done to 'Britain' or the 'United Kingdom' and to describe all the bad things as 'English'.

We do not subscribe to these views. *England's Glory* is an unashamed celebration of England and the English. And we believe that the English have much of which to be proud.

A recent survey showed that English citizens were responsible for four out of five of the world's great inventions and discoveries. Books about the world's greatest thinkers, scientists, artists and industrialists invariably include more individuals born in England than anywhere else.

Any list of the world's greatest thinkers must include Francis Bacon, John Stuart Mill, John Locke, Thomas Malthus and Thomas Hobbes. The names William Shakespeare, Charles Dickens, John Milton, Daniel Defoe and Geoffrey Chaucer would head any list of the world's greatest writers. An all-time list of the world's top dozen scientists would have to include Charles Darwin (the father of the theory of evolution), Michael Faraday (who gave us electricity and the electric motor), Charles Babbage (who invented the computer), William Harvey (who discovered the circulation of the blood), Joseph Lister (who saved millions of lives by introducing antiseptic procedures into surgery), John Snow (the first real epidemiologist and the doctor who made anaesthetics acceptable), Joseph Swan (who invented the electric light bulb) and Charles Wheatstone (who invented the telegraph and the telephone).

A list of innovators and originators would have to include George Cayley (the originator of manned flight), George Stephenson (the inventor of the railway), William Henry Fox Talbot (the inventor of photography), Robert Hooke (whose list of important inventions would fill a book), William Petty (the father of modern economics) and many, many more. Any world list of influential politicians would have to include Oliver Cromwell (the father of parliamentary democracy), Robert Peel (who introduced the world's first police force) and Rowland Hill (the father of the Post Office and the postage stamp). No list of explorers and adventurers would be complete without Francis Drake, Walter Ralegh (also spelt Raleigh) and James Cook.

Many of the great English achievements have been airbrushed out of the history books. Time and time again credit for new inventions is claimed dishonestly and inappropriately. (The Americans are, we fear, particularly guilty of this.) It is time for a little pride and joyful flag-waving. And that is what this book is all about.

Vernon Coleman and Donna Antoinette Coleman

P.S. For the purposes of this book 'English' means born in England.
P.P.S. One of the authors of this book, Donna Antoinette, is half Welsh and half English. It was her English half which wrote her half of *England's Glory*.
P.P.P.S. Traditionally, the English measure in 12s (or dozens) rather than 10s, and so the lists in this book are in dozens and half-dozens.

ABBEYS

England's Dozen Most Magnificent Abbeys

1. Westminster Abbey, London – Westminster Abbey was consecrated in 1065. The present Gothic-style abbey dates largely from the reign of King Henry III who, having chosen it as his burial site, had it knocked down and rebuilt. Westminster Abbey is the final resting place of many celebrated kings and queens. Also, it is the setting for State funerals and coronations. William the Conqueror was the first monarch to be crowned there in 1066.

2. Tewkesbury Abbey, Gloucestershire – Building of the present Abbey began in 1102. Tewkesbury Abbey is famous around the world for its medieval architecture, monuments and magnificent stained glass. At 148ft tall, the 12th century tower of Tewkesbury Abbey is the largest in England.

3. Rievaulx Abbey, Yorkshire – St Bernard of Clairvaux sent 12 monks from Clairvaux in France to found the Abbey in 1132. Rievaulx Abbey, which was once home to some 150 monks and 500 lay brethren, was the first Cistercian abbey in northern England.

4. Fountains Abbey, Yorkshire – England's largest monastic ruin was founded in 1132 by 13 reforming monks from the Benedictine St Mary's Abbey, York. Until Henry VIII's Dissolution of the Monasteries, Fountains Abbey was one of the richest and most influential Cistercian abbeys in the whole of England.

5. Battle Abbey, Sussex – Founded in 1070 by William the Conqueror, on the site of the Battle of Hastings. The high altar of the original building (sadly, little remains of the original structure) was built on the site where King Harold fell in battle, and is now marked by a plaque. The best feature of the abbey

is the very impressive looking Great Gatehouse, which was rebuilt in 1338.

6. Malmesbury Abbey, Wiltshire – Founded in 676 by St Aldhelm. In 1005, Elmer, the flying monk, jumped off the abbey's tower (with wings fastened to his hands and feet) to see whether he could fly. Luckily, he survived the 200ft drop but did break both his legs. He decided that he couldn't fly.

7. Romsey Abbey, Hampshire – In 1544, the people of Romsey paid Henry VIII £100 so that they could carry on using part of the building, which was allocated to them, as their parish church. Romsey Abbey was built in the 12th century to replace the nunnery that had been destroyed by the Vikings.

8. Shrewsbury Abbey, Shropshire – Founded in 1083 by the Earl of Shrewsbury, Roger de Montgomery. It began life as a small, wooden chapel of St Peter until the resident priest – having returned from a pilgrimage to Rome – persuaded Montgomery to turn the building into a magnificent abbey.

9. Lacock Abbey, Wiltshire – Founded in the early 13th century by the Countess of Salisbury as a nunnery of the Augustinian order. Lacock Abbey lies in its own woodland grounds in the heart of the village of Lacock. William Henry Fox Talbot, the inventor of photography, lived here. And the first photograph ever taken was of one of the Lacock Abbey windows.

10. Buckfast Abbey, Devon – Founded in 1018 during the reign of King Cnut, and was rebuilt in stone when it became a Cistercian abbey in 1147. Sadly, the building was left to ruin after the Dissolution of the Monasteries by King Henry VIII. However, it was re-founded in 1882, by some Benedictine monks who had been exiled from their own monastery in France. Restoration of the abbey church, which was created by the monks themselves, began in 1907 and was completed in 1938. When work began on the abbey church, there was a rule that no more than six monks worked on the building at any one time. Today, Buckfast Abbey is still active and the monks lead lives not dissimilar to the monks who lived there nearly a thousand years ago.

11. Whitby Abbey, Yorkshire – The majestic remains of Whitby Abbey stand tall on a headland overlooking Whitby town. St

Hilda founded the original abbey on the site in 657. Sadly, the original abbey was completely destroyed by the Danish invasion in 867. The remains visible today date from around 1220.

12. Glastonbury Abbey, Somerset – It was once one of the wealthiest abbeys in England. The alleged graves of King Arthur and Queen Guinevere were found by the monks in 1191. The abbot's kitchen is one of the best-preserved medieval kitchens in Europe.

ANGEL OF THE NORTH

1. The 65ft tall Angel of the North was created by artist and former Turner Prizewinner, Antony Gormley, and was completed in 1998.

2. This beautiful, weather-resistant corten steel sculpture stands close to the A1 at Gateshead.

3. The Angel of the North has a staggering 177ft wingspan.

4. The Angel of the North is built to withstand winds of up to 100 miles per hour. To prevent it from blowing over in high winds, the sculpture is anchored by 500 tons of concrete foundations.

5. The body of the Angel of the North is hollow, allowing for internal inspections. Its access door is on one of its shoulder blades.

6. The wings are 3.5 degrees forward and not flat, to create 'a sense of embrace'.

ANIMALS IN WAR

The English love animals and to ensure that the courage and ingenuity of animals in wartime is never forgotten there is now a special animal memorial in London.

The Animals in War Memorial (unveiled by Princess Anne in 2004) in Central Park Lane, London, is a memorial to all animals who suffered and perished in wars. The provision of the memorial was inspired by author Jilly Cooper.

The inscription on the memorial reads: 'This monument is dedicated to all the animals that served and died alongside British and Allied forces in wars and campaigns throughout time. They had no choice.'

ARISTOCRACY

'*The English aristocracy may seem to be on the verge of decadence, but it is the only real aristocracy left in the world today. It has real political power through the House of Lords and a real social position through the Queen. An aristocracy in a republic is like a chicken whose head has been cut off: it may run about in a lively way, but in fact it is dead. There is nothing to stop a Frenchman, German or Italian from calling himself the Duke of Carabosse if he wants to, and in fact the Continent abounds with invented titles. But in England the Queen is the fountain of honours and when she bestows a peerage upon a subject she bestows something real and unique.*'

'*The great distinction between the English aristocracy and any other has always been that, whereas abroad every member of a noble family is noble, in England none are noble except the head of the family. In spite of the fact that they enjoy courtesy titles, the sons and daughters of Lords are commoners – though not so common as baronets and their wives who take precedence after honourables.*'

(NANCY MITFORD, ON 'THE ENGLISH ARISTOCRACY' FROM HER BOOK *NOBLESSE OBLIGE* 1956)

AUSTEN, JANE (1775-1817)

Much loved English novelist, Jane Austen, is known for her elegant style of writing, her irony, wit and the uncanny perceptions of minor landed gentry and country clergy that she expressed in her widely read novels.

Daughter of a rector, Jane Austen was born on 16 December 1775 in Steventon, Hampshire. Jane Austen was one of eight children. Her sister, Cassandra, who was several years her senior, was Jane's best friend and confidante. Cassandra, who never married, survived her sister by 28 years.

Although Jane Austen received some outside schooling, she was primarily educated at home by her father and older brothers.

Jane Austen started her writing when she was a young girl to amuse her family and friends, and wrote *Love and Friendship* (which was published as recently as 1922) when she was only 14-years-old. Jane Austen's novels include, *Sense and Sensibility* (1811), *Pride and Prejudice* (1813), *Mansfield Park* (1814), *Emma* (1816), *Persuasion* and *Northanger Abbey*. Her last two novels were published posthumously in 1818. *Sense and Sensibility* was published at Jane Austen's own expense. During her lifetime, Jane Austen's novels were published anonymously because at that time, writing was not considered to be a lady-like occupation.

Jane Austen never married. However, she did enjoy a short youthful flirtation with a good-looking, young man called Tom Lefroy. Jane Austen even accepted a marriage proposal, which she changed her mind about the following day, to a 21-year-old heir called Harris Bigg-Wither; she was 26 at the time.

At just 41-years-old, Jane Austen died on July 18, 1817 from what was for a long time believed to have been Addison's disease, although recent evidence suggests that she might have died from Hodgkin's disease. Jane Austen was buried in Winchester Cathedral.

At the time of her death, Jane Austen was working on another novel called, *Sandition*, but died before completing it.

BACON, FRANCIS (1561-1626)

Bacon was a scholar, essayist, historian, scientific author, lawyer, philosopher and politician. He was a proud and intensely patriotic Englishman and is generally accepted by philosophers and historians around the world as the father of modern science. Here are half a dozen facts about Francis Bacon:

1. Bacon's first major book was his collection of essays (entitled, appropriately, *Essays*) which first appeared in 1597. These essays are penetrating reflections on human nature and conduct; the work of an experienced observer.

2. It is Bacon's writing on the philosophy of science that defines his greatness most vividly and it was his book the *New Instrument* which truly changed the world. Up until Bacon, scientists and other thinkers had relied upon the system of deductive logic espoused by Aristotle. But Bacon realised that we only gain new knowledge by observing the world, collecting facts and then using inductive reasoning to draw conclusions from our collected facts. Bacon believed that the scientist should act as an interpreter of nature and that knowledge can only be derived from experience and experiments. He believed that experiments had to be carefully planned and that the resulting evidence had to be carefully assessed. Only when the facts had been obtained, he believed, should conclusions be drawn.

3. Bacon's 'big idea' was that the systematic examination of the facts was the first thing to be done in any scientific investigation and that until this had been done, faithfully and impartially, with all the safeguards that experience and forethought could suggest, all generalisations, all anticipations from mere reasoning, had to be adjourned or postponed.

4. Bacon spoke with clear authority and he persuaded future generations that the patient, intelligent, persevering cross examination of facts, and careful study and assessment of the results, was the only way to obtain worthwhile knowledge. He worked on this idea for 40 years and wrote about it many times. This may all sound obvious to us now. But in the 17th century it

was not at all obvious and it was not the way most men thought. Bacon believed that if men followed his plan, there were no bounds to what human thought could accomplish.

5. Bacon was no great scientist. But, in his own words, he rang the bell which called scientists to order. He was the father of modern science and modern philosophy. His great contribution to science was to create the idea of empirical thought – the principle that we should build up our knowledge by using our senses to observe what happens around us (whether it is happening by accident or because of something – an experiment – we have devised). Ever since Bacon's time, all good scientists, in countries all around the world, have followed the English method as created and codified by Francis Bacon. When the Royal Society of London was founded in 1662, the founders named Francis Bacon as their inspiration. And although he was no scientist, Francis Bacon never avoided a chance to experiment. It was an experiment which killed him.

6. In March 1626, he climbed out of his coach on a freezing cold day in Highgate and collected snow for an experiment on preserving food in cold storage. He bought a hen from an old woman, and had her kill it, and he then stuffed the dead hen with snow. Suspecting that meat might be as well preserved in snow as in salt, he wanted to observe the effect of cold on the preservation of flesh. He was 65-years-old and frail and he caught a chill. He was taken to a nearby house where he was put into a damp bed. The result was that a few days later he died of bronchitis. He did, however, live long enough to see that his experiment had worked.

BACON'S SAYINGS

Half a Dozen Quotes from Francis Bacon's Essays:

1. 'Young men are fitter to invent than to judge, fitter for execution than for counsel, and fitter for new projects than for settled business;...Men of age object too much, consult too long, adventure too little...Certainly it is good to compound

employments of both…because the virtues of either age may correct the defects of both.'

2. 'A crowd is not company, and faces are but a gallery of pictures, and talk but a tinkling cymbal where there is no love.'

3. 'Riches have wings and sometimes they fly away of themselves, sometimes they must be set flying to bring in more.'

4. 'Some books are to be tasted, others to be swallowed, and some few to be chewed and digested.'

5. 'A little philosophy inclineth a man's mind to atheism, but depth in philosophy bringeth man's mind about to religion.'

6. 'Money is like mulch – not good except it be spread.'

BADMINTON

In 1863, the eighth Duke of Beaufort's children invented a game to overcome their boredom during the winter months. This game was referred to by guests to the Duke's house as 'that Badminton game'. For it was at Badminton House in Gloucestershire that the Duke and his family lived.

BANGERS AND MASH

Few meals are more 'English' than bangers and mash. A plateful of bangers and mash consists simply of good quality sausages and mashed potato with plenty of onion gravy. The nickname 'bangers' for sausages dates back to wartime rationing. The sausages were, at that time, filled with so much water that they exploded when they were fried.

BASEBALL

Baseball was invented in England – not America. In 1744, the game (originally base ball) was first named and described in a very popular book called *A Little Pretty Pocket Book*.

BIG BEN
Two Dozen Facts

1. The world famous clock tower, Big Ben, stands at the end of the Houses of Parliament and is 316ft tall.

2. In 1834, fire destroyed the old Palace of Westminster and, thus, the present Houses of Parliament came into existence along with Big Ben.

3. The clock's mechanism was designed by Edmund Beckett Denison QC. Edward Dent constructed the clock's mechanism until his death in 1853, then his stepson, Frederick Dent, completed his stepfather's work.

4. The clock was originally built to help time parliamentary debates.

5. Big Ben was originally the name used for the clock's main bell but soon became the name for the whole clock tower.

6. The construction of the clock tower for Big Ben began in 1843, and Big Ben was started officially on 31 May 1859. The hourly strike wasn't introduced until 11 July 1859, and the quarter chimes were introduced two months later.

7. The hourly note of the bell is 'E natural'. There is a crack just under 1ft long in the great bell that occurred just weeks after the bell came into operation. It is the crack that gives Big Ben its unique tone.

8. The hammer that strikes the great bell weighs four cwts.

9. Big Ben can be heard as far as four and a half miles away.

10. The clock is wound by an electric motor. The clock was wound by hand until 1913. Winding the clock used to take 30 hours a week.

11. The tune of Big Ben's chimes is based on a passage in the aria *I Know That My Redeemer Liveth* from Handel's *Messiah*.

12. Big Ben is thought to be named after the Chief Commissioner of Works of that period, Sir Benjamin Hall. Sir Benjamin was affectionately nicknamed 'Big Ben' because of his large girth and height (he was 6ft 4in). However, some believe Big Ben to be named after the heavyweight prizefighter of that era, Ben Caunt. Ben Caunt's nickname was also Big Ben.

13. The official name for the bell in Big Ben is the Great Bell.

14. The Great Bell carries the following inscription: '*The bell weighing 13 tons 10 cwt 3 qrs 15 lbs was cast by George Mears of Whitechapel for the clock of the Houses of Parliament under the direction of Edmund Beckett Denison Q C in the twenty-first year of the reign of Queen Victoria and in the year of Our Lord MDCCCLVIII*'.

15. There are 334 steps to the top of Big Ben, and 290 steps to the clock room.

16. The clock tower contains a prison cell. The cell was last used in 1880. Members of parliament (MPs) used to be imprisoned there if they were found guilty of a breach of parliamentary privilege. The suffragette, Emmeline Pankhurst, was held for a short time in the cell.

17. Big Ben's chimes have been used on the BBC since 1924.

18. The clock, which has four dials, is renowned for its accurate timekeeping. Big Ben is the most consistently accurate public clock in the world and strikes its first blow for each hour to within a second of the time.

19. Greenwich Mean Time became the legal standard throughout the British Isles in 1880. Before 1880, public clocks around Britain had their own local time which wasn't always the same as that shown by Big Ben.

20. There are 312 glass panes in each of Big Ben's four dials. The south dial was shattered during an air raid in 1941 but the accuracy of the clock was unaffected.

21. The hour hands of Big Ben are made of gunmetal. The minute hands are made of copper. The hour hands are 9ft long and the minute hands are 14ft long.

22. Over the years, the clock has stopped on several occasions due to birds, workmen, bad weather, etc. But the most serious occasion was in August 1976 when metal fatigue caused severe damage to the clock, resulting in Big Ben's chimes falling silent. The clock didn't chime again until May 1977 in time for the Queen's visit to the Palace of Westminster for her Silver Jubilee.

23. On 12 August 1949, a group of starlings slowed down the clock by 5 minutes after landing on one of the minute hands.

24. Since 1885, a lantern above the clock's belfry has been lit whenever the Commons is in session after dark. The lantern is known as the 'Ayrton Light' after the man whose idea it was, Acton Ayrton, who was MP and Commissioner of Works during the 1870's.

BLACKPOOL TOWER
A Dozen Facts

1. Blackpool Tower, which was inspired by the Eiffel Tower in Paris, was finished in 1894. It was Blackpool's mayor, John Bickerstaffe, who had the idea for building the Blackpool Tower after he had seen the sensational new Eiffel Tower at the Paris Exhibition.

2. The 518ft high tower comprises 93 tons of cast iron and 2,493 tons of steel. Maxwell and Tuke of Lancashire were the architects. Sadly, both Maxwell and Tuke died before the Tower finally opened to the public.

3. On a clear day, it is possible to see the Isle of Man from the Tower Top.

4. In 1897, the top of Blackpool Tower caught fire as a result of an electrical fault.

5. During World War II, Blackpool Tower was nicknamed the RAF Tower as it was used as a Royal Air Force radar station.

6. A staggering 650,000 tourists visit the Tower every year.

7. A post box was placed at the top of the Tower in 1949.

8. It takes seven years to paint the tower from top to bottom. The men who paint Blackpool Tower are nicknamed 'Stick Men'. In celebration of Queen Elizabeth's Silver Jubilee in 1977, the top of the Tower was painted silver.

9. The late comedian, W. C. Fields, spent a season as a circus juggler at Blackpool Tower before he became a Hollywood star.

10. Ten thousand light bulbs are used to illuminate the Tower.

11. In 1929, the first Wurlitzer organ was installed in the Ballroom at the base of the Tower.

12. In 1956, the Ballroom and the restaurant underneath were badly damaged by fire. The Ballroom's dance floor was completely destroyed. It took two years to repair the damage.

BOWLER HAT

In 1849, William Coke, a relative of the Earl of Leicester, approached well-known hatters, Lock & Co. of St James's Street, London, and asked them to design a tight fitting, hard hat that would protect his gamekeepers' heads from dangerous poachers and overhanging branches. He wanted the hat to fit tightly so that it could not be easily blown off by the wind. Lock & Co. (founded in 1676 and still in business today) passed on William Coke's requirements to the felt hat makers, Thomas and William Bowler of Southwark Bridge Road in London.

As soon as the hat was ready, William Coke travelled from his Holkham estate in Norfolk to collect it.

When the hat was handed to him, he put it on the floor and jumped up and down on it to see if it could withstand his weight. After this test, satisfied with the new headgear, Coke paid for the hat (which was hardened with shellac) and ordered a dozen.

William Coke (pronounced cook) was the first person in England to own and wear a bowler hat and, in his memory, the bowler hat is sometimes known as a 'coke'.

BREAD AND BUTTER PUDDING

This simple 'classic English dish' with its firm, golden brown crust topping is believed to date back to the early 17th century. The basic ingredients include bread, butter, currants, eggs, sugar and milk. Not wanting to waste bread, the poor would use their stale bread and add fruit or even meat to it, then bake the concoction in the oven.

BREAKFAST

A full English breakfast consists of fried bread, fried eggs, bacon, sausages, fried mushrooms, a fried/grilled tomato, baked beans and a generous helping of tomato sauce or brown sauce. The Full English Breakfast is considered not to be complete unless accompanied by a plateful of freshly-made toast, served with butter and marmalade. The whole meal should be washed down with a mug of hot, milky tea.

BROOKE, RUPERT (1887-1915)

The famous English poet, Rupert Brooke, was born in Rugby, Warwickshire. He died at the age of 27 in World War I in Greece. He wrote the following poem in 1914.

The Soldier

If I should die, think only this of me:
That there's some corner of a foreign field
That is for ever England. There shall be
In that rich earth a richer dust concealed;
A dust whom England bore, shaped, made aware,
Gave, once her flowers to love, her ways to roam,
A body of England's breathing English air,
Washed by the rivers, blessed by the suns of home.
And think, this heart, all evil shed away,

A pulse in the eternal mind, no less
Gives somewhere back the thoughts by England given;
Her sights and sounds; dreams happy as her day;
And laughter, learnt of friends; and gentleness,
In hearts a peace, under an English heaven.

BRONTË, ANNE, CHARLOTTE AND EMILY

The three Brontë sisters, daughters of a widowed clergyman, lived on the bleak Yorkshire moors with only their imaginations for comfort. They all died young but among them they wrote some of the best-known novels in the English language. Charlotte (1816-1855) was the first born and the last to die. She was only 38-years-old when she died but her novels included *Jane Eyre*, *Shirley* and *Villette*. Emily was born two years later than Charlotte and died in 1848 at the age of 30. Her only novel was *Wuthering Heights*. The third sister, Anne, was born in 1820 and died in 1949. Her novels included *Agnes Grey* and *The Tenant of Wildfell Hall*. Both Charlotte and Anne died of tuberculosis.

BROWNING, ROBERT (1812-1889)

Robert Browning, one of England's most famous poets, was born in London and died in Venice.

Home-thoughts from Abroad

O to be in England
Now that April's there,
And whoever wakes in England
Sees, some morning, unaware,
That the lowest boughs and the brushwood sheaf
Round the elm-tree bole are in tiny leaf,
While the chaffinch sings on the orchard bough
In England – now!
And after April, when May follows,

And the whitethroat builds, and all the swallows!
Hark, where my blossom'd pear-tree in the hedge
Leans to the field and scatters on clover
Blossoms and dewdrops – at the bent spray's edge -
That's the wise thrush; he sings each song twice over
Lest you should think he never could recapture
The first fine careless rapture!
And though the fields look rough with hoary dew,
All will be gay when noontide wakes anew
The buttercups, the little children's dower -
Far brighter than this gaudy melon-flower!

BRUNEL, ISAMBARD KINGDOM (1806-1859)

A Dozen Facts

1. Isambard Kingdom Brunel, renowned as a genius working in iron, was born in Portsmouth, Hampshire, the son of the engineer Sir Marc Brunel.

2. The young Brunel's first job was taking full charge of the Thames Tunnel being dug at Rotherhide. He was just 20-years-old at the time. The building of the tunnel nearly cost the young Brunel his life because he was injured when the tunnel flooded and he spent six months recuperating.

3. At the age of 26, Isambard Kingdom Brunel was appointed Engineer to the newly created Great Western Railway. The bridges, tunnels and stations he planned are still used today by modern high speed trains travelling between London and Bristol and his bridges now safely carry trains which are ten times as heavy as anything Brunel envisaged.

4. The Great Western Railway is a magnificent tribute to Brunel's genius. Paddington Station in London is a Brunel creation and there is an excellent statue to him beside Platform 1. Brunel's Box Tunnel, which was the longest railway tunnel in the world at the time, is orientated so that the rising sun shines all the way through it on Brunel's birthday.

5. Brunel was so meticulous that he even designed the specification for the locomotives to be used on his railway.

6. Throughout his remarkably short life, Brunel continued to build railways. He built lines in Ireland, Italy and Bengal.

7. Brunel saw the railway from London to Bristol as the first step in creating a link between London and New York, and to complete the link he subsequently built ships to cross the ocean.

8. The 'Great Western' was the first real ocean-going steamship ever built and the 'Great Britain' was the first large ship to be driven by screw propellers. The third huge ship he built, the 'Great Eastern', had an unprecedented five funnels and was so big that it remained the largest ship on the seas for half a century. Each vessel was a major step forward in ship building. The 'Great Eastern' played a vital part in laying the first lasting transatlantic telegraph cable in 1865.

9. Brunel's other work included tunnels, buildings, viaducts and docks. His notebooks and sketchbooks show that he involved himself in every detail of his creations. For example, he surveyed the entire length of the railway route between London and Bristol himself.

10. For the Crimean War, Brunel designed a hospital of prefabricated parts that could be shipped out to the Crimean and reassembled on the battlefield. The hospital arrived complete with its own drainage system and its own air conditioning. He even designed new guns for use in the war.

11. The Clifton Suspension Bridge, 700ft long and 200ft above the River Avon, had the longest span of any bridge in the world when it was built. It still stands today and carries over four million vehicles each year. The Royal Albert Bridge, at Saltash in Cornwall, is another lasting monument to Brunel's genius.

12. Brunel's designs revolutionised the world of engineering and public transport. Sadly, he endured years of ill health before dying of a stroke at the tragically early age of 53. Few men have achieved so much in so little time.

BRUNEL'S DOZEN MOST MAGNIFICENT ACHIEVEMENTS

1. Paddington Station, London. Iconic railway station.
2. SS 'Great Western', pioneering transatlantic steam ship.
3. South Devon Railway. Brunel's railway running along the coast at Dawlish in Devon is one of the most dramatic and best-loved stretches of railway line in the world.
4. Clifton Suspension Bridge, across Avon Gorge, Bristol. Finished in 1859 as a monument to the man recognised as the greatest engineer of all time.
5. Bath Spa Railway Station.
6. Royal Albert Bridge.
7. Bristol Temple Meads Railway Station.
8. SS Great Britain, in her day the biggest ship in the world.
9. Tamar Bridge – a 730 yards long construction which enabled railway travellers to reach Cornwall.
10. The Great Eastern steam ship set standards for the future of shipbuilding.
11. Box Tunnel, carrying Great Western Railway through Box Hill.
12. Maidenhead Bridge.

BUCKINGHAM PALACE

A Dozen Facts

1. Buckingham Palace takes its name from the house that was built there by Tory politician, John Sheffield, in the early 18th century. John Sheffield, who was a friend of Queen Anne, was created Duke of Buckingham in 1703. Queen Anne gave him part of St James's Park so that he could expand his estate.
2. In 1761, George III bought Buckingham House for his wife, Queen Charlotte.

3. In 1821, the architect John Nash began the reconstruction of Buckingham House as a neo-classical palace for George III's son, George IV. Unfortunately, George IV died before the Palace was completed. And sadly, George IV's successor, William IV (who decided not to live at the palace), did not allow John Nash to finish the reconstruction because he wanted a cheaper architect. It was the architect Edward Blore who finished the building. It was Sir James Pennethorne (John Nash's nephew) who added the south wing, which includes the massive ballroom (the largest room in the Palace) and the state supper room.

4. The ballroom was opened with a ball in 1856 to celebrate the end of the Crimean War.

5. Queen Victoria was the first sovereign to live in the 'new Buckingham Palace' after her coronation in 1837.

6. Buckingham Palace has a staggering 775 rooms (that's a lot of curtains). One hundred and eighty eight of the rooms are staff bedrooms. Buckingham Palace has 760 windows, which are cleaned every six weeks.

7. Buckingham Palace is the Queen's official London residence.

8. The Queen and Prince Phillip occupy only one section of one floor of one wing at Buckingham Palace.

9. The Royal Standard flag flies above Buckingham Palace when the Queen is in Residence. When the Queen is not in residence, the Union Flag flies.

10. Buckingham Palace gardens, which extend to about 40 acres, include a lake, a tennis court and a helicopter landing area.

11. Part of Buckingham Palace was bombed during World War II. The palace suffered nine direct bomb hits. One policeman was killed.

12. In 1837, during Queen Victoria's reign, security at the palace was so inefficient that a 12-year-old boy was able to live undetected at the palace for a whole year. Although greatly improved, security at the palace wasn't that efficient nearly 150 years later. In 1982, an Irishman, Michael Fagan, managed to get into Buckingham Palace by climbing over the 14ft wall surrounding the palace and getting past security, despite the intruder alarm

going off twice. Fagan wandered around the palace and found the Queen's bedroom. With his hand bleeding all over the Queen's blankets after breaking a glass ashtray, he refused the Queen's orders to leave and talked to Her Majesty until the police eventually arrived.

BUTLERS

The butler is a quintessential English servant. In large English houses he was the most senior servant. In drawing room murder mysteries it was, traditionally, always the butler who did 'it'. Here is an account of the duties of the butler, as first described by Mrs Beeton in the best-selling book of household advice that bears her name:

'The domestic duties of the butler are to bring in the eatables at breakfast, and wait upon the family at that meal, assisted by the footman, and see to the cleanliness of everything at table. On taking away, he removes the tray with the china and plate, for which he is responsible. At luncheon, he arranges the meal, and waits unassisted, the footman being now engaged in other duties. At dinner, he places the silver and plated articles on the tables, sees that everything is in its place, and rectifies what is wrong. He carries in the first dish, and announces in the drawing-room that dinner is on the table, and respectfully stands by the door until the company are seated, when he takes his place behind his master's chair on the left, to remove the covers, handing them to the other attendants to carry out. After the first course of plates is supplied, his place is at the sideboard to serve the wines, but only when called on.

The first course ended, he rings the cook's bell, and hands the dishes from the table to the other servants to carry away, receiving from them the second course, which he places on the table, removing the covers as before, and again taking his place at the sideboard.

At dessert, the slips being removed, the butler receives the dessert from the other servants, and arranges it on the table, with plates and glasses, and then takes his place behind his master's chair to hand the wines and ices, while the footman stands behind his mistress for the same purpose, the other attendants leaving the room. Where the old-fashioned practice of having the dessert on the polished table, without any cloth, is still adhered to, the butler should rub off any marks made by the hot dishes before arranging the dessert.

Before dinner, he has satisfied himself that the lamps, candles, or gas-burners are in perfect order, if not lighted, which will usually be the case. Having served every one with their share of the dessert, put the fires in order (when these are used), and seen the lights are all right, at a signal from his master, he and the footman leave the room.

He now proceeds to the drawing-room, arranges the fireplace, and sees to the lights; he then returns to his pantry, prepared to answer the bell, and attend to the company, while the footman is clearing away and cleaning the plate and glasses.

At tea he again attends. At bedtime he appears with the candles; he locks up the plate, secures doors and windows, and sees that all the fires are safe.

In addition to these duties, the butler, where only one footman is kept, will be required to perform some of the duties of the valet, to pay bills, and superintend the other servants. But the real duties of the butler are in the wine-cellar; there he should be competent to advise his master as to the price and quality of the wine to be lain in; 'fine', bottle, cork, and seal it, and place it in the binns. Brewing, racking, and bottling malt liquors, belong to his office, as well as their distribution. These and other drinkables are brought from the cellar every day by his own hands, except where an under-butler is kept; and a careful entry of every bottle used, entered in the cellar-book; so that the book should always show the contents of the cellar.

The office of butler is thus one of very great trust in a household. Here, as elsewhere, honesty is the best policy: the butler should make it his business to understand the proper treatment of the different wines under his charge, which he can easily do from the wine-merchant, and faithfully attend to it; his own reputation will soon compensate for the absence of bribes from unprincipled wine-merchants, if he serves a generous and hospitable master. Nothing spreads more rapidly in society than the reputation of a good wine-cellar, and all that is required is wines well chosen and well cared for; and this a little knowledge, carefully applied, will soon supply.'

Taken from *Beeton's Book of Household Management*.

CARROLL, MADELEINE

Madeleine Carroll (the female star of Hitchcock's classic movie *The 39 Steps*), was born in West Bromwich. During the Second World War, she gave up acting and became a Red Cross nurse. She turned her Chateau in France into an orphanage. She was awarded the Legion d'Honneur by France and the Medal of Freedom by the USA.

CARS

An Englishman (Richard Trevithick) invented, built and drove the first car. Motor sport originated in England. It is, therefore, hardly surprising that the English love cars. Here are the names of a dozen Classic English car manufacturers:

1. Aston Martin
2. Austin
3. Bentley
4. Bristol
5. Jaguar
6. Jenson
7. Lagonda
8. MG
9. Morgan
10. Rolls Royce
11. Triumph
12. Wolseley

CASTLES

England's Dozen Most Magnificent Castles

1. Windsor Castle, Berkshire (residence of the Queen) – The original structure was founded by William the Conqueror. Windsor Castle has been the chief residence of English sovereign since the reign of Henry I in the 12th century, and is the largest occupied castle in the world.

2. The Tower of London (home to the Crown Jewels) – The central keep (known as the White Tower) was first begun in 1078 by William the Conqueror. During its long life the Tower of London has been a palace, a prison, a zoo, a treasury and an arsenal.

3. Warwick Castle, Warwickshire – This magnificent, classic castle stands tall over the River Avon. It was William the Conqueror who built the original motte and bailey fort. During the 18th century, the wonderful grounds were re-landscaped by 'Capability Brown'.

4. Leeds Castle, Kent – Built by Robert De Crevecoeur in 1119. In 1278, the castle became a royal palace for King Edward I and his wife, Eleanor of Castile. After Queen Eleanor of Castile, Leeds Castle was held consecutively by five more medieval queens.

5. Arundel Castle, West Sussex – Founded at the end of the 11th century. For over 800 years, Arundel Castle has been in the family of the Duke of Norfolk. Queen Victoria and Prince Albert visited Arundel castle for several days in 1846.

6. Berkeley Castle, Gloucestershire – Situated on the east side of the Severn, part of Berkeley Castle dates back to Norman times. Sadly, this beautiful castle, surrounded by wonderful Elizabethan terraced gardens, is haunted by a gruesome incident. In 1327, King Edward II was held captive and later murdered at Berkeley Castle.

7. Kenilworth Castle, Warwickshire – One of England's glorious ruined castles. Visited by Queen Elizabeth I on three separate occasions. Over the centuries, John of Gaunt, Henry V and Robert Dudley (the Earl of Leicester) are among those who

played a part in the building and re-modelling of Kenilworth Castle.

8. Ludlow Castle, Shropshire – One of the first Norman castles to be built entirely of stone. The first Tudor King, Henry VII, spent much of his early life here.

9. Bamburgh Castle, Northumberland – It was the first English castle to be badly damaged by cannon fire. There had been previous settlements on the site of Bamburgh Castle since prehistoric times.

10. Warkworth Castle, Northumberland – It began as a Norman motte and bailey and developed into a large fortress. The castle contains a largely intact eight-towered, three-storey keep.

11. Dover Castle, Kent – This 900-year-old castle was surrendered to William the Conqueror by Harold of England. On the same site 2,000 years previously, there had been an Iron Age fort. At Dover Castle there is a lighthouse and lookout-point which the Romans erected.

12. Tintagel Castle, Cornwall – Very little remains of this castle today but we've included it on our list because King Arthur is said to have been born there. And it is, supposedly, where the Knights of the Round Table met and planned their adventures.

Note: A keep is the strongest or central tower of a castle. A motte is a mound which forms the site of a castle. A bailey is the outer wall of a castle.

CATHEDRALS
England's Dozen Most Magnificent Cathedrals

1. York Minster, Yorkshire – The present building was begun around 1230 and wasn't completed until 1472. It is England's largest gothic cathedral. With 128 windows, York Minster cathedral contains a vast collection of medieval stained glass. The Great East Window of the cathedral is the largest example of medieval stained glass in the whole of England and, indeed,

the whole of the world. Around 2 million pieces of glass make up the cathedral's 128 stained-glass windows.

2. Wells Cathedral, Somerset – Situated in the smallest city in England, the spectacular facade of medieval figure carvings on the west front of Wells Cathedral makes it the finest in England. It was the first medieval building to have pointed arches.

3. St Paul's Cathedral, London – The most famous of all English cathedrals. Rebuilt by Christopher Wren after the Great Fire in 1666 destroyed Old St Paul's. This magnificent cathedral took 42 years to build.

4. Canterbury Cathedral, Kent – Contains amazing 13th century stained glass, which depicts fascinating stories of Christian life. In 1170, Archbishop of Canterbury, Thomas à Becket, was murdered in Canterbury cathedral by four of King Henry II's knights.

5. Lincoln Cathedral, Lincolnshire – This beautiful cathedral has been plagued by disaster. In 1141, the 11th century original was destroyed by fire. Then it was destroyed by an earthquake in 1185. In 1548 the spire blew down. (Up until that point it was the world's tallest building.)

6. Salisbury Cathedral, Wiltshire – At 404ft tall, Salisbury Cathedral's spire is England's tallest. One of only four existing copies of the Magna Carta can be seen at Salisbury cathedral.

7. Durham Cathedral, Durham – Built between 1093-1133 as a resting place for St. Cuthbert. At the west end of the cathedral is Galilee Chapel (added around 1170) which contains the tomb of Venerable Bede.

8. Peterborough Cathedral, Cambridgeshire – The west front of the cathedral has three, deep and very large arches, creating a very striking effect. The cathedral provides the final resting place for Henry VIII's first wife, Catherine of Aragon.

9. Lichfield Cathedral, Staffordshire – The only medieval cathedral in England with three spires. Its three beautiful spires are nicknamed 'The Ladies of the Vale'.

10. Worcester, Cathedral, Worcestershire – It has the earliest Perpendicular central tower; completed in the 1370s. The music

of the great English composer, Edward Elgar, is associated with this cathedral. He lived close by. A window and a plaque at the cathedral commemorate the great composer.

11. Winchester Cathedral, Hampshire – Famous for its chantry chapels, the Norman cathedral was begun in 1079. Jane Austen's tomb rests at Winchester Cathedral.

12. Coventry Cathedral, Warwickshire – The ruined nave and spire of the 15th century St Michael's Cathedral _ destroyed by bombs during World War II – stands next to the new cathedral which was consecrated in 1962. Coventry Cathedral contains some spectacular works of art.

CHAMPAGNE

The French invariably claim to have invented champagne. Indeed, the European Union has given France the rights to the 'methode champenoise'. No wine maker living outside the limited Champagne region of France is allowed to use the name 'champagne' to describe their produce.

But the French didn't invent champagne.

Champagne was invented by a self-taught English scientist called Christopher Merrett who came from the cider-producing West Country. Born in 1614, Merrett devised two techniques which were fundamental for manufacturing champagne; and he did it decades before the Benedictine monk Dom Perignon who is usually given the credit for inventing the most luxurious of luxury wines.

Merrett used techniques from the cider industry to control the second fermentation process which makes wine fizzy.

It was in 1662 that Merrett gave a scientific paper to the Royal Society in London in which he described adding vast quantities of sugar and molasses to wine made it taste 'brisk and sparkling'.

It wasn't until 30 years later that Dom Perignon's work at the Abbey of Hautvillers at Epernay officially started the vast champagne industry.

It was also Merrett who invented the stronger glass which is needed to stop the bottle exploding when it contains champagne.

In a publication entitled *The Art of Glass* he explained how bottles could be made stronger by adding iron, manganese or carbon to the molten mixture. Early French champagne makers recognised Merrett's contribution and described the bottles they used as being made of verre Anglais (English glass).

CHANGING OF THE GUARD AT BUCKINGHAM PALACE
Half a Dozen Facts

1. The Changing of the Guard ceremony, which takes place on the forecourt of Buckingham Palace, involves new guards coming on duty to replace the ones who are going off duty.

2. Seven army regiments (including the two regiments of the Household Cavalry – the ones who are on horses) have the responsibility of guarding the Monarch. Together they form the Household Division.

3. The Foot Guards – instantly recognisable by their smart red tunics and bearskin hats – are infantry soldiers from any of the following five regiments in the British Army: the Coldstream Guards, the Grenadier Guards, the Irish Guards, the Scots Guards and the Welsh Guards.

4. You can tell which regiment Foot Guards belong to by the buttons on their tunics. The Welsh Guards wear their buttons in fives; the Coldstream Guards wear their buttons in twos; the Irish Guards wear their buttons in fours; the Scots Guards wear their button in threes; and the Grenadier Guards have single buttons. The Foot Guards also have different collar badges. For example, the Irish Guards' collar badge is a shamrock. Another way of being able to identify which regiment the Foot Guards belong to is by their bearskin hats. Four out of five varieties of bearskin hat are adorned with a plume (the exception, without a plume, is the bearskin of the Scottish regiment). The plumes are worn either on the left-hand side or on the right-hand side. Each regiment has a different coloured plume.

5. The Changing of the Guard on the forecourt of Buckingham

Palace takes place at 11.30 a.m. every day. During the autumn and winter the ceremony takes place on alternate days (weather permitting).

6. The Changing of the Guard is accompanied by a Guards' band. The music played includes traditional military marches, songs from musicals and films, and popular tunes.

CHARACTERS IN ENGLISH FICTION
England's Dozen Greatest (together with their creators)

1. James Bond (Ian Flemming)
2. Bertie Wooster (P. G. Wodehouse)
3. Jeeves (P. G. Wodehouse)
4. David Copperfield (Charles Dickens)
5. Mr Pickwick (Charles Dickens)
6. Little Nell (Charles Dickens)
7. Miss Marple (Agatha Christie)
8. Scrooge (Charles Dickens)
9. Mr McCawber (Charles Dickens)
10. Jane Eyre (Charlotte Brontë)
11. Lord Emsworth (P. G. Wodehouse)
12. Robinson Crusoe (Daniel Defoe)

CHAUCER, GEOFFREY
(C. 1343-1400)

Geoffrey Chaucer was extremely well-connected and lived as full a life as a man can live if he's not Lord Byron. He worked as a spy, an ambassador and a controller of customs. He was also a prolific author. Most of his work was written to be read out loud at court and in the homes of rich noblemen.

He started work on his epic work *The Canterbury Tales* in 1387, when he was in his 40s, though the *Tales* weren't available in a printed version until William Caxton printed them in around 1478.

The Canterbury Tales is a collection of stories supposedly told among a band of merry pilgrims who are entertaining themselves as they make their way to the shrine of Thomas à Becket in Canterbury.

In the prologue, Chaucer describes the character of pilgrims such as the Wife of Bath, the Pardoner, the Knight and so on. He planned 120 separate tales but had finished only 22 (and started 2 more) when he died.

The stories (difficult to read in the original Olde Englishe) vary enormously in style and content – according to which of the pilgrims is telling them. Some of the stories are serious, religious and filled with philosophical thoughts. Some are romantic. And some are comic, rude and, on occasion, downright dirty. Some are gloomy, some are uplifting and some are merely entertaining.

The Canterbury Tales marked the beginning of English literature.

CHEESE

The French think they are the only nation to make cheese. They aren't, of course. The English have been making cheeses for centuries. Here are half a dozen favourite English cheeses:

1. Cheddar cheese – A ploughman's lunch in an English pub just wouldn't be the same without a big slice of Cheddar cheese (and a dollop of pickle of course!). Cheddar cheese has been produced from around 1170, and is the most popular cheese in England (and the world!). This natural white to pale yellow, firm-textured cheese originated from a town called Cheddar in Somerset. Traditionally, Cheddar cheese had to be produced within 30 miles of Wells Cathedral.

   The cheese has to be kept at a constant temperature for maturing (14 months or more for vintage Cheddar). Caves provide a perfect environment. The caves at Wookey Hole and Cheddar Gorge are still used for the maturation of some Cheddar cheeses.

According to local legend, Cheddar cheese was discovered after a milkmaid had accidentally left her milk pail in the caves at Cheddar Gorge. When the milkmaid later returned to collect her pail she found that the milk inside resembled something rather different. She sampled it, and found that it had a rather distinctive but pleasant taste and, thus, Cheddar cheese was born.

The 'father of Cheddar cheese' – 19th century dairyman, Joseph Harding – was responsible for the modernisation and standardisation of Cheddar cheese with his promotion of dairy hygiene, unremunerated propagation of modern cheese-making techniques and for his technical developments. Joseph Harding introduced his 'revolving breaker' for curd cutting. His method was the first modern system for producing Cheddar based upon scientific principles. Joseph Harding was responsible, more than any other person, for making Cheddar cheese popular all around the world.

West Country Farmhouse Cheddar has been awarded the Protected Designation of Origin (PDO) status. This means that it has to undergo a process of rigorous auditing. To comply with the PDO rules, West Country Farmhouse Cheddar has to be hand-cheddared and made from local milk in one of four counties: Somerset, Devon, Dorset or Cornwall. The cheese has to be matured in the place where it was made for at least nine months and must not contain any colouring, flavouring or preservatives.

2. Stilton – England's favourite blue cheese is known as 'The King of Cheeses'. Stilton was first produced in the early 18th century in and around Melton Mowbray in Leicestershire. The cheese acquired its name from the village of Stilton about 80 miles north of London even though the cheese had never been produced there.

3. Cheshire – This dense, crumbly, semi-hard cheese is one of the oldest recorded cheeses in English history with a mention in the *Domesday Book*. Originally, Cheshire cheese was the generic name for cheese produced in the county of Cheshire and parts of the surrounding counties.

4. Red Leicester – Red Leicester (formerly known as Leicestershire Cheese) was named after the county from which it originated. It was made on Sparkenhoe Farm in Upton by Mr George Chapman in 1745. A natural plant dye called annatto gives the cheese its orange colour.

5. Gloucester – There are two types of Gloucester cheese: single and double. Single Cloucester is made from skimmed milk from the evening milking combined with a small amount of whole milk from the morning milking. Double Gloucester is made from just whole milk from the morning and evening milking. Both types of Gloucester are usually produced in round shapes. Double Gloucester cheese is used in the annual cheese-rolling event on Cooper's Hill near Gloucester.

6. Lancashire – This cheese can be traced back as far as the 13th Century. Lancashire cheese can be classified as tasty, creamy or crumbly. Crumbly Lancashire was first created in the 1960s, but Tasty Lancashire and Creamy Lancashire are the traditional Lancashire cheese styles. These cheeses have been produced using the same method for over 100 years. Lancashire County Council employee, Joseph Gornall, helped create a formal method and recipe, and standardised Lancashire Cheese production across the county. Creamy Lancashire is considered the ideal cheese to have on toast, because it does not become stringy when melted.

CHILDREN'S PASTIMES

A Dozen Traditional English Pastimes for Children

1. Conkers
2. Bowling a hoop
3. Lighting a fire with a magnifying glass
4. Skimming flat stones over water
5. Playing Pooh sticks on a stream
6. Climbing a tree
7. Looking in rock pools

8. Building a sandcastle on a beach

9. Whittling a stick with a penknife

10. Making a daisy chain

11. Making a bow and arrow

12. Collecting driftwood/shells, etc. on a beach

CHILDREN'S BOOKS

Most of the world's most popular writers of books for children were born in England. Here are a dozen English children's authors together with their most famous books or creations:

1. Lewis Carroll (*Alice's Adventures in Wonderland*)

2. Enid Blyton (*Famous Five*)

3. Charles Kingsley (*The Water-Babies*)

4. Hugh John Lofting (*Dr Dolittle*)

5. Beatrix Potter (*The Tale of Peter Rabbit*)

6. Anna Sewell (*Black Beauty*)

7. Frances Burnett (The Secret Garden)

8. Frank Richards (Billy Bunter)

9. A. A. Milne (Winnie the Pooh)

10. Anthony Buckeridge (Jennings and Darbishire)

11. Captain W.E. Johns (Biggles)

12. J. K. Rowling (Harry Potter)

CHURCHILL, WINSTON (1874-1965)

Churchill was archetypically English and although he had his faults (arrogance and vanity to name but two) it was his good fortune (and ours) that he was able to turn his faults into virtues and to use his self-confidence to enhance his qualities as a leader. He was a lucky leader and a lucky man; a born survivor. Not many people change the course of history single-handedly. Churchill did. Churchill, the ultimate egoist and self-publicist changed history. If it hadn't been for World War II he would be no more than a political blip. But if it hadn't been for Churchill, Hitler might well have won World War II.

Churchill may not have been a great statesman or a great politician. He was too opinionated, too pugnacious and too obviously self-centred (other politicians are equally driven by self-interest but they hide it more effectively). But he was the greatest warrior, the greatest war time leader any country has ever produced and the greatest orator. That's quite enough for one man.

Here are three dozen facts about Winston Churchill:

1. English politician and author, Sir Winston Churchill, was born two months premature on 30 November 1874 at Blenheim Palace, Oxfordshire. His full name was Winston Leonard Spencer Churchill. Winston Churchill's father (the third son of the 7th Duke of Marlborough) was Lord Randolph Churchill. At the age of 37, Lord Randolph was leader of the House of Commons and Chancellor of the Exchequer. Churchill's mother was the beautiful Jennie Jerome, the daughter of a rich American speculator.

2. Churchill's ancestor, the first Duke of Marlborough, was Queen Anne's Captain General. Queen Anne had created him the first Duke of Marlborough in recognition for his military victories. In gratitude, Queen Anne also rewarded the Duke with the Royal Manor of Woodstock, and funded the building of Blenheim Palace – named after the Duke's victorious battle at Blenheim.

3. Churchill experienced a lonely childhood and would often write begging letters to his parents asking them to visit him during his stay at boarding school. Most of the time, his pitiful requests went ignored.

4. The red-haired Churchill was described as a somewhat troublesome child. He was bumptious, wilful, restless and mischievous – personality traits, which some say, never left him.

5. At thirteen, Churchill attended public school at Harrow, and did not do as badly there as he later led many to believe. It is true that he was considered a dunce in some of his subjects, more notably Latin, but in truth he was only poor in the subjects that he did not care for. Winston was brilliant at subjects that interested him, especially English and History. Churchill's father, disappointed and concerned at his son's relative lack of scholarly success, wondered what route his boy's life should take. One day, whilst watching his son at play with his toy soldiers, the idea of a military career for the young Churchill was born. This was good news for Churchill because it was a dream that he had coveted since he was a small boy.

6. Churchill sat his Army preliminary examination at Harrow. The examination involved drawing a map. The evening before the examination, he wrote names of countries on pieces of paper and put them into a hat. He then picked out one to study. The country he blindly chose was New Zealand. In the examination paper the following day, he was asked to draw a map of New Zealand. This was an example of the luck that was to follow him throughout his life.

7. Two popular misconceptions about Churchill were that he was dyslexic and that he suffered from a stutter. Churchill was not dyslexic and he did not have a stutter, though he did have a slight lisp. However, his speech impediment did not deter him from becoming the greatest orator the world has ever seen.

8. In 1893, Churchill left school and attended the Royal Military Academy, Sandhurst. He graduated from Sandhurst in 1895, having done extremely well, and joined the Fourth Hussars.

9. Impatient with peacetime soldiering and desperate for action, the young Churchill travelled to Cuba while on leave. The fighting between the indigenous rebels and the Spanish Government was finally reaching a conclusive phase. Before he left for Cuba, Churchill arranged a contract with the *Daily Graphic* to write articles about his experiences over there. This was the start of his career in journalism. He was paid £5 for each article. When he left Cuba, Churchill was awarded the Spanish Military Medal (1st Class).

10. In 1896, Churchill was stationed with the Fourth Hussars in Bangalore, India. The following year, during his three months' leave, he got a job as a war correspondent (for the *Daily Telegraph* and the Indian newspaper, *Allahabad Pioneer*) in the north-west frontier of India. Churchill's experiences in north-west India inspired him to write his first book, *The Malakand Field Force*. Winston Churchill went on to become an eminent and prolific author, writing over 40 books.

11. In 1953, Churchill was awarded the Nobel Prize for literature. He started his writing career for financial reasons, and continued writing for financial reasons throughout his life.

12. During his time on leave, while still officially stationed in India, Churchill heard about a pending war to clean up the Sudan. Churchill tried to persuade Lord Kitchener to assign him to his army there, but Lord Kitchener refused. Never a man to give in, the young Churchill enlisted the support of the Prime Minister Lord Salisbury and successfully persuaded the Adjutant General to give him a post in the 21st Lancers. Before setting off for the Sudan, Churchill managed to get a contract as war correspondent for the *Morning Post*. It was on the field of Omdurman on 2 September 1898, that the last classic cavalry charge in the history of British warfare was fought.

13. The war to liberate the Sudan from the Dervishes was successful despite the fact that a quarter of Kitchener's men were killed or wounded. Churchill wrote about the history of the campaign in his next book, *The River War*. In this book, Churchill criticised General Lord Kitchener's policies. The War Office responded by introducing a law restraining the literary freedom of serving soldiers in the British Army. It's a law that still exists.

14. Winston Churchill was one of the very few modern political leaders to have real personal experience of war. He knew what it was like to be shot at and what it was like to be a prisoner of war. His experiences gave him a unique experience as a war time leader.

15. In 1899, Churchill gave up his military career and decided to go into politics. Churchill always believed that he was destined for great things, and told a fellow officer while in Bangalore that

he would one day be Prime Minister. His political career did not start well. He failed to win his first political contest – the by-election at Oldham. So when the *Morning Post*, impressed by his journalistic work during the Sudan, asked him to be chief war correspondent to report on the war with the Boers which was about to break out in South Africa, Churchill jumped at the chance.

16. A British army armoured train on which Churchill was travelling in South Africa was ambushed and partly derailed by the Boers. Unfazed by the bullets firing all around him, Churchill took charge of the situation and managed to direct the engine (which was still on the rails) to safety, having first loaded the train with wounded men. He later wrote to his mother and said: 'Bullets are not worth considering. Besides I am so conceited I do not think the gods would create so potent a being for so prosaic an ending'.

17. When Churchill returned on foot to help the remaining men, he was captured and taken to a prisoner of war camp in Pretoria. A little less than a month later, Churchill managed to escape from the camp. He travelled just under 300 miles to safety. When his escape was discovered, a 'Dead or Alive' price was put on Churchill's head with a £25 reward. Churchill's escapades made him a hero for a while in Britain.

18. After his escape from Pretoria, Churchill did not return to London but, instead, went to Durban to rejoin the army commanded by General Sir Redvers Buller. At Durban, Churchill received a hero's welcome. General Buller wanted to enrol Churchill into the forces, but Winston didn't want to lose his job with the *Morning Post* so instead he accepted an offer of a commission in The South African Light Horse. This meant that he could be a soldier and continue as a highly paid war correspondent.

19. Churchill was present at the battle of Spion Kop (where he intervened and took over the role of commanding officer) and was among the first to arrive in Ladysmith and Pretoria, before resigning his commission and returning to Britain in July 1900. He was just 24 years old.

20. In 1900, Churchill again stood as a Conservative Party candidate for Oldham during the general election. This time, he was

successful. His election victory was no doubt helped by his fame as a military hero. As a politician, Churchill quickly proved himself to be a champion of the underdog. He spoke out about poverty in Britain and on the 31 May 1904, dissatisfied with the policies of the Conservatives (especially their proposed protective tariffs on foreign trade, which he was against), and believing that the policies of the Liberals were more like his own, he caused quite a stir when he crossed the floor of the House of Commons to join the Liberals.

21. In 1905, when the Liberals formed a Government, Churchill was appointed Under-Secretary of State for the Colonies. Sir Henry Campbell-Bannerman was Prime Minister. Churchill was appointed President of the Board of Trade when Liberal leader, Campbell-Bannerman was succeeded by Herbert Henry Asquith in 1908. As President of the Board of Trade, Churchill helped introduce legislation which transformed society. He set up Labour Exchanges and established minimum wages for several hundred thousand workers. He also proposed unemployment insurance.

22. On 12 September 1908, Winston Churchill married Clementine Hozier, whom he had met at a dinner party six months previous. They had five children together: one son and four daughters. They named their son, Randolph, after Sir Winston's father. In contrast to his own father, Churchill was an affectionate and attentive father to all of his children.

23. In 1910, Churchill was promoted to Home Secretary, becoming the youngest in the post since Robert Peel. One of his first actions was to introduce the Coal Mines Bill, which made it illegal for children under 14 to work underground. During his time as Home Secretary, Churchill caused much criticism when he famously took charge of the Sidney Street siege in London's East End, and forced the criminals to surrender or burn by denying the fire brigade access when the house they were in caught fire.

24. After a year as Home Secretary, Churchill became the political head of the navy: First Lord of the Admiralty. He helped

to strengthen the British fleet in order to deter Germany's aggression. He introduced aircraft into the Royal Navy.

25. During the First World War in 1915, Churchill unfairly received the lion's share of the blame for the ill-fated Gallipoli landings on the Dardenelles. As a result, he was demoted to the post of Chancellor of the Duchy of Lancaster. (The Conservatives had refused to form a coalition government with the Liberals unless Churchill was demoted.) Soon after, Churchill resigned from the Government (although he remained an MP) and rejoined the army. He served in the trenches on the Western Front for several months, first with the Grenadier Guards and then as Commanding Officer of the 6th Battalion Royal Scots Fusiliers.

26. In 1916, Prime Minister Asquith resigned from the coalition Government and was replaced by the English-born professional Welshman, David Lloyd George. In 1917, Lloyd George appointed Churchill his Minister of Munitions and, in 1919 (after the First World War ended) Churchill was made Secretary of State for War. Two years later, in 1921, Churchill set up a conference in Cairo to settle Mesopotamia's future.

27. Lloyd George resigned as Prime Minister in 1922, and the Conservatives withdrew from the coalition government. The Conservatives returned to power in the 1922 general election after an interval of 17 years. Churchill, recovering from an appendicectomy found that he was without a parliamentary seat, for which he famously said he was: 'without an office, without a seat, without a party and without an appendix'.

28. In the first month of 1924, the Conservatives were defeated in Parliament, and Ramsay MacDonald became the first Labour Party Prime Minister of Britain. In the same year, the Conservatives offered Churchill the safe seat of Epping – a constituency that he represented for 40 years. In October, the Conservatives won the General Election and Stanley Baldwin appointed Churchill as Chancellor of the Exchequer, a position that his father had held almost 40 years earlier. As Chancellor of the Exchequer one of the many things Churchill did was introduce pensions for everyone at 65 and reduce Income tax for the lowest income groups.

29. In 1929, the Conservatives were defeated in the General Election, and Labour came into power with Ramsay MacDonald as Prime Minister. Churchill was relegated to the back benches. During the next few years, which he described as his 'wilderness years', Churchill concentrated on writing. He resigned from the Shadow Cabinet because of his strong stance against Indian Home Rule. During his time out of office, Churchill called on Britain to strengthen itself against Germany as he saw the rise of Adolf Hitler as a threat. His warnings were ignored.

30. In September 1939, on the day the Second World War started, the Prime Minister Neville Chamberlain appointed Churchill First Lord of the Admiralty and in May 1940, when Chamberlain resigned after having been blamed for a number of defeats during the beginning of the war, Churchill was made Prime Minister. He was 65 years old.

31. In his first speech as Prime Minister of the coalition government Churchill famously said: 'I have nothing to offer but blood, toil, tears and sweat'. Churchill's impassioned speeches were a great inspiration to many during the war and helped to raise the nation's morale.

32. On the 8 May 1945, Churchill brought Britain to victory against Germany. Despite Churchill's leadership during World War II, he was heavily defeated in the 1945 election by Clement Attlee and the Labour Party.

33. Churchill, 76-years-old, returned as Prime Minister of the Conservative Party after Labour's defeat in the 1951 General Election. Two years later, in 1953, Churchill was made Knight of the Garter.

34. Churchill stepped down as Prime Minister on 5 April 1955, but he continued to remain a Member of Parliament until six months before his death.

35. Sir Winston Churchill, the famous Havana cigar smoking British statesman and author, died on 24 January 1965. He was given a State Funeral and was buried in St Martin's Churchyard, Bladon. When Churchill's coffin passed down the Thames, the cranes of London's docklands bowed in salute.

36. Churchill was a successful painter. He exhibited and sold his works

at public exhibitions in Britain and France under the pseudonym of 'Charles Morin'. Churchill saw several of his works exhibited in the Royal Academy under the name of 'Charles Winter', and, later, had several more in the Royal Academy under his own name. Churchill was also an accomplished bricklayer. He took it up as a hobby during his time as Chancellor of the Exchequer. He built some of the buildings on his estate at Chartwell.

CHURCHILL, WINSTON – QUOTES

1. 'I have nothing to offer but blood, toil, tears and sweat.' (*Churchill's first speech at the House of Commons on becoming Prime Minister, 13 May 1940*)
2. 'Victory at all costs, victory in spite of all terror, victory however long and hard the road may be; for without there is no survival'. (*House of Commons 13 May 1940*)
3. 'We shall not flag or fail. We shall go on to the end, we shall fight in France, we shall fight on the seas and oceans, we shall fight with growing confidence and growing strength in the air, we shall defend our island, whatever the cost may be. We shall fight on the beaches, we shall fight on the landing grounds, we shall fight in the fields and in the streets, we shall fight in the hills; we shall never surrender...' (*House of Commons, 4 June 1940*)
4. 'Let us therefore brace ourselves to our duties, and so bear ourselves that, if the British Empire and its Commonwealth lasts for a thousand years, men will still say, 'This was their finest hour.'' (*Speech at the House of Commons referring to the Dunkirk evacuation, 18 June 1940*)
5. 'The battle of Britain is about to begin.' (*House of Commons, 1 July 1940*)
6. 'Never in the field of human conflict was so much owed by so many to so few.' (*Speech at the House of Commons referring to the Battle of Britain pilots, 20 August 1940*)
7. 'Give us the tools and we will finish the job'. (*Radio broadcast, 9 February 1941*)

8. 'Now this is not the end. It is not even the beginning of the end. But it is, perhaps, the end of the beginning.' (*Speech at Mansion House referring to the Battle of Egypt, 10 November 1942*)

9. 'The Almighty in His infinite wisdom did not see fit to create Frenchmen in the image of Englishmen.' (*House of Commons, 10 December 1942*)

10. 'Perhaps it is better to be irresponsible and right than to be responsible and wrong.' (*Party Political Broadcast, London, 26 August 1950*)

11. 'Everyone has a right to pronounce foreign names as he chooses.' (*The Observer, 'Sayings of the Week' 5 August 1951*)

12. 'To jaw-jaw is better than to war-war'. (*Speech in Washington, 26 June 1954*)

CLOTHES

A Dozen Items of Classic English Clothing for Men

1. Bow tie
2. Club tie
3. Brogue shoes
4. Waistcoat
5. Tweed suit
6. Cravat
7. Pinstripe suit
8. Deerstalker (hat) with ear flaps
9. Smoking jacket
10. Bowler hat
11. Trilby hat
12. Wellington boots (black)

Khaki, knee-length shorts (worn in hot climates, together with a knotted handkerchief placed on top of the head) are a modern addition to the Englishman's wardrobe.

A Dozen Items of Classic English Clothing for Women

1. Twin set (a cardigan worn over a matching jumper, usually with a single string of pearls)
2. Tweed suit
3. Brogue shoes
4. Waxed jacket
5. Tweed skirt
6. Headscarf
7. Shawl
8. Trench coat
9. Wellington boots (green)
10. Knee-high boots
11. Miniskirt
12. Pinafore

COBBETT, WILLIAM (1763-1835)

Author, journalist, publisher, campaigner, social historian, politician and rebel – it's difficult to sum up William Cobbett who was, without a doubt, one of the most determined, bloody-minded and brave Englishmen who ever lived. He wrote what he believed and didn't give a hang for the consequences.

He believed that England had a personality and that it needed and deserved a genuine 'England' policy. He believed it was important to preserve the personal peculiar characteristics of England and to respect the special individual liberties enshrined in the nation's history and culture. He believed that a popularly elected Parliament, representing an informed democracy, would end the borough mongering and the sinecures which, in his day, still disgraced public life.

Cobbett was blisteringly honest, forever shrewd and wrote without fear or favour. He had a singular talent for arousing passion among his readers. It was, and could have only been, Cobbett who, protesting about the social costs and consequences of the industrial revolution, claimed that England was building her industrial dominance on the backs of 30,000 little girls. Here are two dozen facts about William Cobbett:

1. William Cobbett, born the son of a farmer and inn-keeper, was self-educated. He left home without telling his parents and took a job at Kew Gardens. On the way to Kew he bought a copy of Swift's *Tale of a Tub* with his very last threepence. It was a book he always treasured.

2. After numerous adventures Cobbett found himself a job as a lawyer's clerk in London. He was 21 and hated it. 'No part of my life has been totally unattended with pleasure,' he wrote, 'except the eight or nine months I passed in Gray's Inn.'

3. Bored and despairing he went to Chatham and joined the marines. He taught himself grammar and became clerk to the garrison commandment.

4. In 1785, Cobbett travelled to Nova Scotia and New Brunswick with his regiment, the 54th Foot, quickly rising through the ranks to become a sergeant-major.

5. In 1791, he returned to England, married, and blotted his copybook as a soldier by accusing officers from the 54th Foot of embezzlement. He quickly realised that the authorities were on the side of the officers and so he fled to France. From there he went to Philadelphia. He stayed in America for eight years, teaching English to French refugees and while there he wrote and published an English grammar for French students. He also wrote pamphlets denouncing the French Revolution.

6. It was while in America that Cobbett started publishing pro-English pamphlets. In 1795, he started to use the pseudonym Peter Porcupine and issued *The Political Censor*, a report of proceedings in Congress together with a commentary. He wrote *Life and Adventures of Peter Porcupine* as a defence of his views. He published *Porcupine's Gazette and Daily Advertiser* to denounce the French and advocate an English Alliance.

7. Cobbett hadn't been living in America long before he once again got into trouble, this time for describing the American Government as: 'the most profligately dishonest that I have

ever seen or heard described...the most corrupt and tyrannical that the world ever knew.' He was heavily fined for a libel on Benjamin Rush and left America in dudgeon.

8. When he got back to London in 1800, Cobbett started his own newspaper *The Porcupine*. He campaigned against the weaknesses of the proposed peace with the French.

9. In 1802, Cobbett launched a weekly newspaper called *Cobbett's Political Register*, which he continued to write, edit and publish until his death in 1835. The *Register*, which started off with Tory views and gradually drifted towards more radical opinions, grew to achieve a massive circulation.

10. Wherever there was Cobbett, there was always trouble. He was fined for attacking a Ministry for its conduct of Irish affairs and his house was attacked by a mob. He founded *Cobbett's Parliamentary Debates* (a publication which was later taken over by Hansard).

11. By 1805, Cobbett had enough money to buy a farm. But he continued to write and published constantly; taking an active part in national politics and campaigning against bribery and on behalf of ordinary citizens who were, he felt, getting a pretty raw deal from the politicians. He campaigned vociferously for parliamentary reform and, inevitably, continued to get into trouble.

12. In 1810, he was sentenced to a fine of £1,000 (an enormous sum at the time) and two years imprisonment for an article reporting the flogging of mutinous militiamen. Sent to Newgate prison, he continued to write his weekly newspaper and wrote *Paper Against Gold*, condemning paper money and calling for the National Debt to be abolished and gold to be reintroduced as the nation's only currency.

13. Upon his release from prison, in 1812, Cobbett began to attack the system of tithes. He also wrote *Letter to the Luddites* in an attempt to dissuade labouring men from violence. He reduced the price of his newspaper from one shilling and a halfpenny to twopence. The circulation and authority soared.

14. Cobbett wrote scathing comments about 'pocket boroughs' and 'rotten boroughs'; complaining viciously about the way

that parliamentary seats could be bought or handed over to 'favourites'. He also attacked the way that corruption and bribery affected the decisions of MPs. He raged about the 'sinecurists, placemen and taxeaters' who took from the country but never gave anything back in return. He complained bitterly about fiat money. Cobbett pointed out that 'it is the Government's job to help keep us safe, healthy and happy'. 'It is,' he wrote, 'the chief business of a government to take care that one part of the people do not cause the other part to lead miserable lives.'

15. None of this went down any better with the 19th century establishment than it would have gone down with the present day establishment, and in 1817 the Government suspended the Habeas Corpus Act so that it could imprison, without trial, anyone whom it regarded as undesirable. Everyone knew that the suspension of the Habeas Corpus Act was done specifically to get at author (and self-publisher) William Cobbett.

16. Cobbett's enemies even started a journal entitled *Anti-Cobbett*. Rightly fearing the Government's intentions, Cobbett absconded and fled first to France and then to America where he took a farm on Long Island. He didn't return to England until things had quietened down a little. He continued to direct the *Political Register* and wrote and published *A Year's Residence in the United States of America* and *A Grammar of the English Language*.

17. While in the USA, Cobbett dug up the body of Thomas Paine, taking the bones back to England to bury them there. (The bones remained in Cobbett's possession until his death when they were mislaid. He had never got round to reburying them.)

18. In 1820, Cobbett was back in England. The Government introduced a stamp duty on periodicals in an attempt to close down his publications. He stood for Parliament at Coventry but was defeated. He became bankrupt.

19. Cobbett next wrote and published a number of books including *Cobbett's Monthly Sermons* and *Cottage Economy*. In 1830, he reprinted portions of his *Register* under the title *Cobbett's Twopenny Trash*.

20. In 1831, he was indicted on a charge of encouraging disorder. He conducted his own defence and the prosecution failed. This

was the last attempt by the Government to coerce the press by legal action. Cobbett's victory was a real victory for journalism and for the people.

21. Cobbett published *State Trials* and wrote several other books on economics and other subjects. Somehow he managed to find time to run farms too; first in Hampshire and then in Surrey.

22. In 1829, Cobbett published his book *Advice to Young Men* and in 1830 Cobbett published the book for which he is now probably best known, *Rural Rides*, an astonishing and revealing social document which also happens to be an immensely readable account of his horseback adventures around the country. Both were first published as part of his *Register*.

23. In 1832, Cobbett became MP for Oldham. He spoke frequently. He continued to write and publish and to represent Oldham as an MP until his death in 1835.

24. William Cobbett, author, editor and publisher, made many enemies throughout his life. But he also made many people think. Cobbett was one of the greatest Englishmen of all time. Cobbett was an original; he fought for journalism against authority and, with John Wilkes, was the originator of the modern concept of the 'free press'. During the early 19th century, writers were transported, imprisoned and fined without limit. Around 500 publishers were imprisoned in one six year period when Cobbett was operating. Cobbett forced the government to allow writers and publishers more freedom. Cobbett's work was read by millions during his life. Thousands followed his coffin when he died. Cobbett himself said that his popularity was 'owing to giving the truth in clear language'. No writer can, or should, aim higher.

COBBETT, WILLIAM (QUOTES)

William Cobbett is one of the most under-estimated of all Englishmen. A loyal, kind man he was intensely proud of being English and fought like a tiger to protect and improve the lot of the ordinary English working man. Few men have done more for their country, and their countrymen, than William Cobbett. Here are a dozen quotes from some of his books. Although these words were written in the 18th and 19th centuries they bear reading still for Cobbett's words provide a sound commentary on our society and our way of life.

1. 'All that I can boast of in my birth is that I was born in Old England.' (*The Life and Adventures of Peter Porcupine*)

2. 'Our religion was that of the Church of England, to which I have ever remained; the more so, perhaps, as it bears the name of my country.' (*The Life and Adventures of Peter Porcupine*)

3. 'I learned grammar when I was a private soldier on the pay of sixpence a day. The edge of my berth, or that of the guard-bed, was my seat to study in; my knapsack was my book-case; a bit of board, lying on my lap, was my writing-table; and the task did not demand any thing like a year of my life. I had no money to purchase candle or oil; in winter time it was rarely that I could get any evening-light but that of the fire, and only my turn even of that. And if I, under such circumstances, and without parent or friend to advise or encourage me, accomplished this undertaking, what excuse can there be for any youth, however poor, however pressed with other business, or however circumstanced as to room or other conveniences? To buy a pen or a sheet of paper I was compelled to forego some portion of food, though in a state of half-starvation; I had no moment of time that I could call my own; and I had to read and to write amidst the talking, laughing, singing, whistling and brawling of at least half a score of the most thoughtless of men, and that too in the hours of their freedom from all control. Think not lightly of the farthing that I had to give, now and then, for ink, pen or paper! That farthing was, alas, a great sum to me! I was as tall as I am now; I had great health and great exercise. The whole of the money not expended for us at market was twopence a week for each man. I remember, and well I may, that upon occasion I, after all absolutely necessary expenses, had, on a Friday, made shift to have a half-penny in reserve, which I had destined for the purchase of a red-herring in the morning; but, when I pulled

off my clothes at night, so hungry then as to be hardly able to endure life, I found that I had lost my half-penny. I buried my head under the miserable sheet and rug and cried like a child.' (*Rural Rides*)

4. 'All taken together, it seems impossible to find a more beautiful and pleasant country than this, or to imagine any life more easy and happy than men might here lead if they were untormented by an accursed system that takes the food from those that raise it, and gives it to those that do nothing that is useful to man.' (*Rural Rides*)

5. 'From one end to the other of the kingdom Yorkshiremen are looked upon as being keener than other people; more eager in pursuit of their own interests; more sharp and more selfish. For my part, I was cured with regard to the people long before I saw Yorkshire. In the army, where we see men of all counties, I always found Yorkshiremen distinguished for their frank manners and generous disposition.' (*Rural Rides*)

6. 'I could not look up at the spire and the whole of the church at Salisbury without feeling that I lived in degenerate times. Such a thing could never be made now. It really does appear that if our forefathers had not made these buildings we should have forgotten, before now, what the Christian religion was.' (*Rural Rides*)

7. 'Upon beholding the masses of buildings, at Oxford, devoted to what they call 'learning', I could not help reflecting on the drones that they contain and the wasps they send forth! However, malignant as some are, the great and prevalent characteristic is folly: emptiness of head; want of talent; and one half of the fellows who are what they call educated here, are unfit to be clerks in a grocer's or mercer's shop.' (*Rural Rides*)

8. 'But never shall I see another place to interest me, and so pleasing to me, as Bristol and its environs, taking the whole together. A good and solid and wealthy city: a people of plain and good manners; private virtue and public spirit united; no empty noise, no insolence, no flattery; men very much like the Yorkers and the Lancastrians. As to the seat of the city and its environs, it surpasses all that I ever saw.' (*Rural Rides*)

9. 'A national debt, and all the taxation and gambling belonging to it, have a natural tendency to draw wealth into great masses. These masses produce a power of congregating manufactures, and of making the many work at them, for the gain of a few. The taxing government finds great convenience in these congregations. It can lay its hand easily upon a part of the produce; as ours does with so much effect. But the land suffers greatly from this, and the country must finally feel the fatal effects of it.' (*Rural Rides*)

10. 'There is, in fact, no opposition; and this is felt by the whole nation; and this is the reason why the people now take so little interest in what is said and done in parliament, compared to that which they formerly took. This is the reason why there is no man, or men, whom the people seem to care at all about. A great proportion of the people now clearly understand the nature and effects of the system; they are not now to be deceived by speeches and professions. ...The 'gentlemen opposite' are opposite only as to mere local position. They sit on the opposite side of the house: that's all.' (*Rural Rides*)

11. 'The people of England have been famed, in all ages, for their good living; for the abundance of their food and goodness of their attire. The old sayings about English roast beef and plum-pudding, and about English hospitality, had not their foundation in nothing. And, in spite of all the refinements of sickly minds, it is abundant living amongst the people at large, which is the great test of good government and the surest basis of national greatness and security.' (*Cottage Economy*)

12. 'He that eats till he is full is little better than a beast; and he that drinks till he is drunk is quite a beast.' (*Advice to Young Men*)

COCKNEY RHYMING SLANG

According to tradition a true cockney is somebody who is born within the sound of the bells of St. Mary-le-Bow in London. Here are a dozen 'cockney' phrases; together with their meanings:

1. Adam and Eve – Believe
2. Apples and pears – Stairs
3. Bread and honey – Money
4. China plate – Mate
5. Daisy roots – Boots
6. Loaf of bread – Head
7. Mince pies – Eyes
8. Rosy Lee – Tea
9. Ruby Murray – Curry
10. Skin and blister – Sister
11. Saucepan lids – Kids
12. Whistle and flute – Suit

CONSTABLE, JOHN (1776-1837)

The cover of our book is a reproduction of one of England's best-known works of art: 'The Hay Wain' by John Constable. John Constable's greatest love was painting the English landscape, especially around his native home: the valley of the River Stour around Dedham, East Bergholt in Suffolk, an area which is now known as Constable Country. He adored the English countryside. Since his death, Constable's work has gone in and out of fashion with art dealers and collectors. But for Englishmen and Englishwomen everywhere, John Constable, the greatest painter of the English countryside, will always be in fashion.

Incidentally, the word 'wain' is old English for a cart or wagon.

CORNISH LANGUAGE

The Cornish word for Cornish is Kernewek. This beautiful language is directly descended from the ancient language spoken by the Celtic inhabitants of Cornwall and many parts of the British Isles long before the Romans came along and changed everything.

The Cornish language has many striking similarities to the Welsh language and to the Breton language, which is spoken in Brittany in the northwest of France. This is because all three languages are Celtic. For example, 'Merry Christmas' in Cornish is Nadelik lowen. In Welsh it is Nadolig llawen. In Breton it is Nedeleg laouen.

The Cornish language had almost died out in the 18th century (various people claimed that it had died out altogether and that Dolly Pentreath was the last native speaker) but it made a revival before the spoken language was lost altogether. Today, hundreds of people speak fluent Cornish, and this figure is rising all the time. Here are a dozen Cornish words and phrases:

1. Good Morning – Myttin da
2. Good evening – Gorthugher da
3. How are you? – Fatla genes?
4. Please – Marpleg
5. Thank you – Meur ras
6. Goodbye – Dha weles
7. Welcome – Dynnargh
8. Father – Tas
9. It is raining – Yma ow kul glaw
10. Mother – Mamm
11. Cornwall – Kernow
12. Happy New Year – Blydhen Nowydh Da

CORNISH PASTY

The filling inside the crimped, golden pastry casing of a Cornish Pasty consists of chopped beef, sliced vegetables, potato, onion, swede and a touch of seasoning. It is thought that the original pasties contained meat filling in one end and fruit filling in the other. The idea was that Cornish tin miners – who had to stay down the mines during their lunch breaks – could have a two-course meal.

COURAGE (ENGLISH STYLE)

Half a Dozen Examples of English-style Courage:

1. When the Titanic was sinking the band played on.

2. Captain Oates, who sacrificed his life for his companions during Captain Scott's failed expedition. Oates, realising that he was weak and was a burden to his companions, walked out of the tent into an icy blizzard, saying: 'I am just going outside and may be some time.' He was never seen again.

3. After a bomb destroyed the Cabinet Room at 10 Downing Street, where Prime Minister John Major was leading a cabinet meeting, Major said calmly: 'Gentlemen, I think we'd better adjourn to another room.'

4. When Thomas More was about to be beheaded in 1535 he spoke calmly to the warder accompanying him up the steps of the wobbly scaffold. 'I pray thee, see me safely up, as for my coming down, I can shift for myself.' He then added, 'Pluck up thy spirits, man; be not afraid to do thine office; my neck is very short.' He then moved his beard from the block, saying that it had never been found guilty of treason, and prayed God to send the King good counsel.

5. Admiral Horatio Nelson walked about on his ship Victory, wearing all his medals. He did this knowing that he would be a target for enemy sharpshooters but believing that his appearance on deck would encourage his own sailors. He was shot dead by a French sniper.

6. John Major, asked what he was going to do after losing an election replied: 'I'm off to the Oval cricket ground. I will just be in time for the afternoon session of play.'

COVENT GARDEN, LONDON

Covent Garden in London is now famous for the Royal Opera House and a number of shops and restaurants. But the area acquired its name in the 16th century when the monks of Westminster Abbey grew vegetables there. The name stuck after Henry VIII dissolved the monastries and the vegetable garden disappeared. The land became a residential square in 1630. The original Covent Garden theatre was built in 1732 but has twice been destroyed by fire, and rebuilt. Covent Garden square was the site of a fruit, flower and vegetable market from 1670 until 1974.

CRICKET LANGUAGE

Cricket has given a good deal of language and folklore to England and the English. The phrase 'not cricket' means that something is not being done decently or honourably. The phrase 'playing with a straight bat' suggests that someone is behaving properly. The phrase 'close of play' denotes the end of the working day. To say that someone has 'bowled a googly' suggests that they have done something unusual and unexpected.

In cricket, the score 111 is known as Nelson. (A score of 222 is known as double Nelson.) The score is thought to be unlucky for English batsmen. There are two theories about why 111 is known as Nelson. The polite theory is that the number refers to three consecutive sea victories (at the battles of Copenhagen, Nile and Trafalgar) which Nelson 'won, won won'. The slightly impolite theory is that the 111 refers to the notion that by the time he died Nelson only had one eye, one arm and one ball. It is not true that he had one eye. It is true that he had one arm. But only Lady Hamilton knew if he had one ball, and she didn't tell.

CROMWELL, OLIVER (1599-1658)

Oliver Cromwell was a brilliant and inspirational leader; a man of action, and a military mastermind. He led the Parliamentary forces to victory in the English Civil War and was the man most responsible for establishing modern parliamentary democracy, first in England and then throughout the rest of the world.

Many great men have ideas, or institute changes, which would have probably surfaced without them – they just happened to be the first to think of them or to be the men in the right position at the right time.

Cromwell was different.

If Cromwell had not existed, neither England nor the world would have been the same, for if Oliver Cromwell had never lived it is likely that the parliamentary forces would have lost the English Civil War.

Cromwell's victory in the English Civil War, was a trigger which led to the French Enlightenment and the French Revolution, and to the establishment of democratic governments throughout western Europe and in English colonies such as Australia, Canada and the United States of America.

Here are two dozen facts about Oliver Cromwell:

1. Oliver Cromwell, the father of British Parliament and world democracy, was born on 25 April 1599 in Huntingdon, Cambridgeshire. Oliver Cromwell was a descendant of Thomas Cromwell, who was Henry VIII's Chief Minister.

2. With nine cousins already sitting in Parliament, Cromwell wanted to follow family tradition and in 1628 he was elected as one of two MPs for Huntingdon. A year later, King Charles I dissolved Parliament after he had been refused money to pay for another attack on France.

3. In 1640, Charles I recalled Parliament because he needed financial help with his campaign against the Scots. Cromwell (who had undergone a powerful religious conversion during his time out of Parliament) was back in Parliament. From now on, Cromwell's religious beliefs influenced every decision he ever made; like all Puritans he believed the purpose of life was to work hard and to serve God and he was convinced that he was being guided to carry out God's will. Many laws were brought in to rid society of what the Puritans deemed as evil; things which distracted people from worshipping God. Some of the long list of restrictive laws included: no Christmas festivities (for example, mince pies were banned), no travelling on Sundays, no dancing, all theatres to be closed down, no football and so on. It wasn't exactly a fun time.

4. In 1640, after three weeks of Parliament, King Charles again dissolved Parliament after he was refused money for his campaign against the rebelling Scots. Parliament's three-week period after a decade's closure was, not surprisingly, known as the Short Parliament. However, Cromwell wasn't without a parliamentary seat for long for Parliament was recalled later that year (this one was known as the Long Parliament because it lasted in various forms for 20 years).

5. At the end of 1641, the 'Grand Remonstrance' – which Oliver Cromwell supported – was drafted by the Long Parliament. This listed a mass of grievances about King Charles's government of both Church and State, and noted a number of recommended reforms. A copy of the document was given to the King who wasn't much taken with it.

6. In January 1642, goaded by his wife Queen Henrietta, the King stormed into the Chamber of the House of Commons, together with his swordsmen, and attempted to arrest the five main MPs who were involved in the drafting of the Grand Remonstrance. Fortunately, the five MPs had been tipped off that the King was coming and had quickly escaped through another door. The MPs were furious that Charles I should dare barge into the House of Commons uninvited. This was the start of the Civil War. (The incident is remembered in the Black Rod ceremony.)

7. Shortly after King Charles's failed attempt to arrest five of his biggest critics, he left London to raise an army to fight Parliament. In August 1642, the King raised his standard at Nottingham: marking the beginning of the First English Civil War. The war was fought between the Cavaliers and the Roundheads (the Roundheads were so called because of their pudding basin haircuts). The Cavaliers, or royalists were mostly Anglican and Catholics and the Roundheads, the supporters of Parliament, were mostly Puritans.

8. In 1642, at 43 years of age, Cromwell was appointed captain in charge of a small group of cavalry (which he raised) in the Parliament's army, which was led by Lord General Essex. On the 23 October 1642, the first major battle was fought at Edgehill in Warwickshire. There being no referee, both sides claimed

victory. A year later Cromwell, who had no previous military experience, was commissioned as a colonel to raise a cavalry regiment in the Eastern Association. Cromwell's regiment was later famously known as the Ironsides. With his regiment, Cromwell managed to suppress a royalist uprising at Lowestoft and recapture Stamford.

9. In 1644, Cromwell was appointed Lieutenant General of the Eastern Association. As Lieutenant General he was able to put his brilliant military ideas into practice and go on to win many notable victories, such as the famous great battle at Marston Moor on 2 July 1644. Not only did Cromwell's success increase his military reputation but it also helped to increase his influence in politics.

10. Cromwell then became Lieutenant General of the New Model Army – England's first national army. Sir Thomas Fairfax, known as Black Tom because of his dark hair and eyes, was Commander-in-Chief. Cromwell went on to help win the last major battle of the First Civil War against the Royalist army at the battle of Naseby in 1645. The year 1646 marked the end of the First Civil War. Around this time, Parliament demanded that most of the New Model Army should be disbanded. Unhappy about this, the soldiers mutinied. Oliver Cromwell was sent by Parliament to army headquarters to discuss how the grievances could be addressed but, unfortunately for Parliament, Cromwell's sympathies lay with the army.

11. At the end of May in 1647, the army kidnapped King Charles and held him in Newmarket under their control. He was then taken to Hampton Court where Parliament and the army debated what to do with him. The debates were known as the 'Putney Debates' because they were held in Putney. If they'd been held in Neasden they would, presumably, have been known as the 'Neasden Debates'.

12. In 1648, the Second Civil War began, and Parliament appealed to Cromwell for help. Cromwell, along with the army, crushed the Royalist Scots at Preston. The King was put into storage on the Isle of Wight. Parliament implored the King to agree to peace talks, but the King wanted time to make a decision. Exasperated

by the King's indecisiveness, Cromwell and Parliament ordered Charles to be taken to Windsor Castle and put on trial for treason. Cromwell, whose name appeared third on the list of signatories, was one of the people who signed King Charles' death warrant.

13. In 1648, very shortly before the regicide, the army replaced Parliament with the Rump Parliament, which consisted mostly of Independents like Cromwell. The following year the monarchy and the House of Lords were abolished by an Act of Parliament, and England was declared a Commonwealth. The biggest threat to the new Commonwealth was the uprising in Ireland and so in the same year, Cromwell was appointed Lord Lieutenant of Ireland and Commander in Chief of the army there. In 1649, Cromwell defeated the Irish.

14. Cromwell was recalled from Ireland and appointed Commander in Chief of the New Model Army for a new war against the Scots who wanted to restore Charles II to the English throne. The Scots were defeated at the battle of Dunbar in 1650 (even though they had twice as many men). The battle at Dunbar is thought to be Cromwell's greatest victory. Cromwell regularly credited his military victories to God's will – firmly believing that he was fighting God's cause.

15. On January 1 1651 at Scone, the Scots crowned King Charles's son – Charles II – King of Scotland. Charles II, along with the Scots, was determined that he should regain the throne that his father once occupied. Realising that his army was greatly outnumbered by Cromwell's, Charles II made his way to the old royalist strongholds on the borders of Wales in an attempt to gather more troops on the way before heading to London. But Cromwell managed to catch up with Charles II and his army at Worcester, and went on to fight a victorious battle against Charles II and his Scottish supporters on 3 September 1651. Cromwell described the battle as his 'crowning mercy'. It was the final battle of the English Civil War.

16. After the battle of Worcester, Charles II fled to France but, before escaping, he hid from the pursuing army up an oak tree. After his restoration to the throne years later, many pubs in England

were re-named the Royal Oak in honour of the tree that had saved Charles II from being captured.

17. In 1653, Cromwell became exasperated with the Rump Parliament and forcibly dissolved it. He marched into the House of Commons, told them what he thought of them all, called in six musketeers from his regiment, dragged the speaker out by his hair and emptied the House of Commons. Cromwell replaced the Rump with the Barebones Parliament (a Parliament of carefully nominated honest men who were known as the Parliament of Saints). The Barebones Parliament collapsed within a year and in 1653, Cromwell became Lord Protector of England, Scotland and Ireland. As Lord Protector, Cromwell was addressed as His Highness Lord Protector and moved into the King's former palace at Whitehall. At Whitehall Palace, Cromwell lived like a King, employing many of King Charles' old servants. Ironically, Cromwell was now leading the life that he had loathed and fought hard against when King Charles I and King Charles II were on the throne.

18. Cromwell had great ambitions to make England great again and he succeeded. His navy defeated the Spanish at the battle of Santa Cruz in the Canary Islands, he gained a foothold in the West Indies, made peace with the French and ended a trade war with the Dutch.

19. In 1657, despite the House of Commons urging him to accept the crown in a document called the 'Humble Petition and advice', Cromwell declined the offer of becoming King of England, Scotland and Ireland.

20. On 3 September 1658, at the age of 59, Oliver Cromwell, Lord Protector of the Commonwealth of England, Scotland and Ireland died, possibly from a malarial-type disease that had recurred. It is believed that the death of his beloved daughter, Elizabeth, less than a month earlier, had not only weakened his spirit but had weakened his body too.

21. Contrary to everything he believed in when he was alive, Cromwell was given a state funeral with no expense spared. His body was laid to rest at Westminster Abbey. A few years later, Charles II was restored to the throne after being invited back

by Parliament. In a typically vindictive gesture, the remains of Oliver Cromwell were dug up and hung from the gibbett. But King Charles II realised that the battle for royal absolutism had been lost. He did not contest the supremacy of parliament.

22. When the foolish James II tried to restore royal absolutism he was thrown out in a bloodless revolution in 1688. The changes made by Cromwell were not, and would never be, reversed.

23. Books and films have traditionally made the more colourful cavaliers the heroes of English history. Cromwell's Roundheads are invariably portrayed as boring dullards – the bad guys. The truth is the opposite. The Cavaliers, all curly wigs, thigh length boots and fancy jackets, were the oppressors, the sheriffs of Nottingham of their day. The Roundheads were the Robin Hoods. Critics have accused Cromwell of being hypocritical, and have pointed out that although he always argued in favour of democracy he did establish a military dictatorship. This is unfair. Cromwell was devoted to the principles of parliamentary democracy and when circumstances beyond his power forced him to take on power that he did not want to take, he insisted that he did so temporarily. When offered the throne of England he refused it. And he refused the offer of a permanent dictatorship.

24. Cromwell, plainly dressed, rather scruffy even, had a 'swollen and reddish' face that was cursed with warts. He was quite an unattractive man but he was never ashamed of his lack of good looks. When Cromwell had his portrait painted he insisted that the painter included his warts in the painting. (This is the origin of the saying 'warts and all'). Cromwell was a moderate and tolerant and passionate man; a sincere campaigner for the people, for religious tolerance and for an England combining a constitutional monarchy with a parliamentary democracy. He was the achetypal English hero: tough and uncompromising but driven by strong ideals and honourable and honest beliefs. Everyone in the world who now lives in a democratic country owes Oliver Cromwell a huge debt.

CROMWELL'S HEAD

The Bizarre Tale of Oliver Cromwell's Head

1. When Charles II was restored to the throne, out of revenge for signing his father's death warrant he had Cromwell's body dug up from his resting place at Westminster Abbey in the January of 1661. After being dug up from his resting place, Cromwell's corpse was taken to the Red Lion pub in Holburn. The next day the body was taken on a sledge through the streets of London to Tyburn. Cromwell's dead body was then hanged by the neck from the gallows for approximately six hours. Cromwell was cut down and beheaded. It took the axeman eight blows to chop off his head. Cromwell's now headless body was then thrown into a lime-pit below the gallows at Tyburn. His head was displayed on a metal spike which was transfixed onto a 20ft wooden pole. The pole stood on the roof of Westminster Hall. Cromwell's head was displayed on the pole for over 20 years.

2. One night, a ferocious storm broke the spike causing Cromwell's head to fall. A sentinel who was on guard duty at the time was nearly hit by Cromwell's head as it landed with a thud by his feet. The soldier took the head home with him and put it up his chimney. On his deathbed, the soldier confessed to his daughter that he had placed Cromwell's head in the family chimney 20 years earlier. The family then sold the head, and in 1710 the head was seen in Du Puy's show of curiosities in London. In 1738, Du Puy died and the head wasn't seen again for approximately 40 years.

3. An unsuccessful comic actor, Samuel Russell who claimed to be a descendant of Oliver Cromwell, then acquired the head. Having failed to sell the head to Cromwell's former college in Cambridge he displayed Cromwell's head on a stall near the Clare Market in London.

4. In 1787, London jeweller, James Cox, bought Cromwell's head for £118. And in 1799, the Hughes brothers bought the head from Cox for £230. They displayed it in a building in Bond Street.

5. In 1815, Josiah Wilkinson of Kent, bought Cromwell's head

from the Hughes family and kept it in a small box to show family, friends and curious visitors.

6. In 1960, the Wilkinson family offered Cromwell's head to his former college in Cambridge so that it could finally be laid to rest. The college gladly accepted the head. Cromwell's head was buried in the grounds of the college on the 25th March 1960.

CROMWELL'S PRANKS

It is difficult to believe but Oliver Cromwell had a 'naughty schoolboy' sense of humour. He loved to play practical jokes on people.

Here are three of the pranks that Cromwell was reputed to have carried out:

1. In 1618, Cromwell deliberately covered his clothes in cattle dung from a nearby field and turned up at his uncle's party. He danced with several ladies and thought it hilarious when he fouled their dresses with smelly cattle dung.

2. Cromwell started an ink fight with his friend, Henry Marten, immediately after signing King Charles's death warrant.

3. In 1657, at his daughter's wedding party, Cromwell enjoyed spoiling the ladies' dresses by throwing drink over them. He also put sweetmeats on some of the guests' chairs before they sat down. And he chased his son-in-law, grabbed his wig and sat on it. We never said he had a sophisticated sense of humour.

CROMWELL AND THE DISSOLUTION OF PARLIAMENT

'At 11.15 am on 20th April 1653, Cromwell entered parliament to dissolve it. After listening to the debate for a time, then beginning to speak in calm tones, he changed to 'a furious manner', walking up and down the House, stamping the ground with his feet and shouting 'with so much passion and discomposure of mind as if he had been distracted'. He said: 'It is time for me to put an end to your sitting in this place, which you have dishonoured by your contempt of all virtue and defiled by your practice of every vice. Ye are a factious crew, and enemies to all good government. Ye are a pack of mercenary wretches and would like Esau sell your country for a mess of potage.' He pointed to individuals, and called them 'whoremasters, drunkards, corrupt and unjust men' adding 'Ye have no more religion than my horse. Ye are grown intolerably odious to the whole nation...Perhaps ye think this is not parliamentary language. I confess it is not, neither are you to expect any such from me...It is not fit that ye should sit as a parliament any longer. Ye have sat long enough unless you had done more good.' When Sir Peter Wentworth protested at such language from one they had 'so highly trusted and obliged', Cromwell retorted: 'Come, come, I will put an end to your prating. Ye are no parliament. I say ye are no parliament. I will put an end to your sitting.' He shouted to Thomas Harrison, 'Call them in', and the musketeers entered. He pointed to the Speaker: 'Fetch him down.' Harrison hesitated: 'The work is very great and dangerous,' then obeyed. Sir Henry Vane protested: 'This is not honest, yea it is against morality and common honesty.' Cromwell: 'Oh Sir Henry Vane, Sir Henry Vane, the Lord deliver me from Sir Henry Vane.' Then, turning to the mace: 'What shall we do with this bauble? Here, take it away.' Then, to the Members: 'I command ye therefore, upon the peril of your lives, to depart immediately out of this place. Go, get ye out! Make haste! Ye venal slaves be gone! Take away that shining bauble and lock up the doors.' By 11.40 the House was cleared and locked. Someone put up a poster: 'This House is to be Lett; now unfurnished.'

From S.R.Gardiner's book *History of the Commonwealth and Protectorate*, first published in 1903.

CUSTOMS AND TRADITIONS
Eccentric English Customs

Many apparently bizarre English customs were started to ward off evil spirits, celebrate the arrival of spring or ensure a good harvest. They often involve a good deal of eating, drinking and merry making. The Church forced many traditional customs to be abandoned, and today's do-gooding, politically correct health and safety obsessed minions are getting rid of more, but some continue to thrive. We have not included the dates on which these events take place for the very good reason that although some of them take place on the same day every year many of them don't. Some are held on specific occasions such as the first Monday after the fourth Sunday in the month, some are held according to religious festivals (which are themselves often moving events) and some are held when it takes everyone's fancy, or when the moon is doing the right things.

January
1. Straw Bear Festival in Whittlesea, Cambridgeshire – A local farmer wearing a costume of straw (which makes him look roughly like a bear if you half close your eyes) is taken through the town in a procession. Rope is tied around the bear which is taken to dance before villagers' houses.
2. Goathland Plough Slot in Goathland, Yorkshire – Long-sword dancers go through the streets and then have a huge roast dinner, with speeches and awards.
3. Wassailing the Apple Tree in Carhampton, Somerset – Villagers arrive at the old apple tree by the Butchers Arms and at 7.30 p.m. a bonfire is lit. Mulled cider and toast are brought out. The Wassailing song is sung and the cider is sprinkled over the tree's roots. The toast is dipped in cider and placed in the branches of the tree.

February
1. Rocking Ceremony in Blidworth, Nottinghamshire – A 400-year-old ceremony is held at the Church of St Mary. The male child born closest to Christmas day in the parish is rocked in an ancient flower bedecked cradle. The baby is then given a bible and carried through the streets.
2. Blessing the salmon nets, Norham, Northumberland – Nets are blessed and boats put out to sea at midnight on February 14th.

March

1. Tichborne Dole in Tichborne, Hampshire – In the 13th century, Lady Mabella announced that the House of Tichborne would fall if villagers were not given bread on Dole Day (March 25). The day got very rowdy in 1796 but when part of the House actually did fall down in 1803 the tradition was rapidly revived.

2. Hare Pie Scramble and Bottle Kicking, Hallaton, Leicestershire – Held on Easter Monday. A hare pie made of beef is blessed by the vicar and shared among the villagers. Three barrels are rolled to the village boundaries.

3. Nutters' Dance in Bacup, Lancashire – Held on Easter Saturday. Locals blacken their faces, put on turbans, red and white kilts, black jerseys, white stockings and shiny clogs and dance across the town all the while tapping out music on wooden discs (known locally as 'nuts') fastened to their knees, waist and palms. (The men in white coats chasing after them are a recent, optional extra.)

4. The Kiplingcotes Derby in Market Weighton, Yorkshire – A horse race which dates back to 1519. The rules say that if the race is ever missed it must stop forever. And so in 1947, despite heavy snowdrifts, a Mr Stephenson from a local farm walked and rode his horse along the course, and in 2001 Ken Holmes defied foot and mouth restrictions to keep the race alive. The Derby is run over the most gruelling course. The runner-up gets a bigger prize than the winner because the runner-up's prize is made up of all the entrance fees.

5. Royal Shrovetide Football Match in Ashbourne, Derbyshire Dales – Held on Shrove Tuesday and Ash Wednesday. Thousands watch and take part in a free for all over three miles through streets and fields. It is the oldest, largest, maddest, longest game of football in the world. The match is between those born north of the River Henmore (the Up'ards) and those born south of it (the Down'ards). Players use specially made hand painted balls and score by standing in the Henmore and tapping the ball three times against a stone. Goals are rare. In 2007, there was one goal scored (at 8.40 p.m. on Shrove Tuesday) but no goals scored on the Wednesday.

6. World Coal Carrying Championships in Gawthorpe, Yorkshire – Held on Easter Monday. Competitors carry 110 lb of coal over a mile to the maypole on the village green.

May

1. 'Obby 'Oss Ceremony in Padstow, Cornwall – Revellers sing to sleeping townsfolk and then as May Day starts the town and the maypole are decorated with ribbons and flowers. A man wearing a scary mask and a big skirt dances around the streets trying to trap pretty girls under his costume.

2. Cheese rolling, in Stroud and Brockworth in Gloucestershire and in Stilton, Cambridgeshire – Held on May 1st (or May Bank Holiday). In Brockworth, cheeses weighing seven pounds are rolled down a 1 in 2 hill and those who catch 'em keep 'em. A large cheese, rolled at full speed, can be extremely dangerous and there are usually some injuries, with the local hospital on stand-by to provide succour to the most badly wounded. (On occasion the winner is trundled off to hospital clutching his cheese.) In Stroud, a cheese is rolled around the church and villagers are welcome to take a bite. In Stilton there is a cheese rolling race around the town.

3. Woolsack Race in Tetbury, Gloucestershire – The annual Wool Sack Race requires entrants to run up Gumstool Hill with a 60lb sack of wool on their backs. Ladies carry a 35lb sack.

4. Garland Day in Castleton, Derbshire – On Oak Apple Day the Garland King and his Lady Consort ride through the town accompanied by a band and morris men. A garland is presented to the King at 6 p.m. and the procession ends at the church.

June

1. Nettle Eating Contest, in The Bottle Inn, Marsham, Dorset – Competitors are given two foot long nettle stalks and the winner is the person with the longest length of empty stalk after one hour. The competition began after a man found a 16ft long stalk of nettle and announced that if anyone could find a longer one he would eat his.

2. Hepworth Feast in Hepworth, Yorkshire – In 1665, a servant, unpacking a box from London, caught the plague from a flea lurking inside a dress and spread it through the town. The Feast, with morris dancing and brass bands, commemorates the end of the plague in the area.

July

1. Love Feast in Alport Castles Farm, Derbyshire – A group of nonconformists met here in the 17th century to worship in secret. The service includes spring water and fruit cake. Straw is placed on the floor.

2. Kilburn Feast in Kilburn, Yorkshire – A four day feast and fair ends with the mock Mayor and his Mayoress (a man in a dress) fining locals for the silliest penalties they can come up with.

3. Swan Upping in Henley-on-Thames, Oxfordshire – Traditionally swans were rounded up for marking in mediaeval times. Today the Queen's swan marker, in a scarlet uniform, uses six traditional rowing skiffs to herd the swans to shore so that he and the Swan Uppers of the Vinters and Dyers can inspect and mark the birds.

August

1. Bosnall Hen Race in Bonsall, Derbshire – A race for any breed of hens, run over a 65ft track. If there is no winner after three minutes the bird nearest the line is the winner.

September

1. Abbots Bromley Horn Dance in Abbots Bromley, Staffordshire – This is a dance which is believed to date back to the Stone Age. Six men (the Deermen) carry reindeer antlers and are accompanied by a Fool and a musician. They then stage mock battles throughout the village.

2. Egremont Crab Fair and Gurning Championships in Egremont, Cumbria – First held in 1267. Originally included cock fighting and bull baiting and the Parade of the Apple Cart. Today it includes fancy dress, wheelbarrow races and gurning competitions.

October

1. World Conker Championships in Ashton, Northants – The winner is placed on the Conker Throne and given a Conker Crown. Competitors must use conkers provided for them by the organisers.

2. Oyster Feast in Colchester, Essex – Richard I handed the fisheries to Colchester in 1189. The feast is held at Moot Hall.

November

1. Tar Barrel Racing in Ottery St Mary, Devon – Started in 17th century. Today, pubs sponsor a barrel each. Each barrel is soaked in tar for weeks and then lit at 4 p.m. on November 5th. Barrels are rolled or carried through the streets until they are destroyed. The event ends in a huge bonfire. To the spectators, watching competitors hoisting lit barrels onto their shoulders and running with them through the streets until they fall apart appears to be the most terrifying and dangerous of all these traditional events.

2. Biggest Liar in the World Competition in Santon Bridge, Cumbria – Started in the 19th century and began when a pub regular, Will Ritson, insisted that he didn't lie but just stretched the truth. Today, competitors have between two and five minutes to demonstrate their ability to lie. Politicians, clergy and members of the legal profession are barred from entry.

3. The Court Leet in Wareham, Dorset – In the four evenings before the final Friday in November a group of Ale Tasters, Bread Weighers, Chimney Peepers, Leather Sealers and Scavengers meet outside pubs to test local produce. They fine publicans if they find faults – fines levied in the form of alcohol. The event ends with a meal at the Black Bear pub paid for by the local lord of the manor

December

1. Tin Can Band in Broughton, Northamptonshire – The Tin Can Band walks through Broughton making as much noise as possible with pots, pans and dustbin lids to frighten away evil spirits.

2. Tolling the Devil's Knell in Dewsbury, Yorkshire – Since the

13th century, the parish church bell has been tolled on Christmas Eve, once for each year of the Christian era. The ceremony now takes over two hours.

3. Christmas Day Dip in Brighton, Sussex and Bournemouth Dorset – Hundreds of people (many in fancy dress), enter the sea and swim and shiver.

There are, of course, some events which are too haphazard to put into a list relying on the normal monthly calendar. So, for example, the villages of Denby Dale, Near Huddersfield in Yorkshire have a ritual which takes place every 20 years or so. (It has occurred 10 times in the last 200 years.) They bake a giant meat and potato pie (which must be bigger than the one baked the last time) to celebrate some national glory. The first was to celebrate the brief recovery from madness of George III in 1788. Others have been baked to mark the end of the Napoleonic threat (1815), the repeal of the Corn Laws (1846), to celebrate Queen Victoria's Golden Jubilee (1887), to celebrate the jubilee of the repeal of the Corn Laws (1896) and, possibly most delightfully of all, to celebrate 200 years of pie making (1988). The most recent pie was baked to welcome in the new millennium. The pie dish for the year 2000 weighed 12 tons and was 40 foot long, 8 foot wide and nearly 4 foot deep. The pie itself contained 3 tons of beef, half a ton of potatoes and 22 gallons of best bitter. It was taken to Pie Field on the back of a 70 foot long wagon and blessed by the Bishop of Wakefield.

Denby Dale isn't the only English town to celebrate events by baking something large. The village of Aughton in Lancashire used to make a huge plum pudding (20 feet long and 6 feet thick) regularly every 21 years but, sadly, they haven't made one since 1886.

And there are some events which take place at more than one venue within an area. The well dressings in Derbyshire are a good example of this. Believed to have started in pagan, pre-Roman, times, possibly as a thanksgiving for the gift of water, and once known as 'well flowering' this wonderful annual custom involves the decorating of springs and wells with growing things. Some civilisations say 'thank you' to the gods by sacrificing animals. The people of Derbyshire say 'thank you' with flowers. Another theory is that the purity of the local water helped preserve the villagers during the Black Death of the mid 14th century. A third theory is that the wells kept flowing during a prolonged drought in the early 17th century. No one knows precisely why they do it but villagers in Derbyshire have been dressing their wells for a long, long time. Clay-filled wooden trays are mounted on wooden frames and a design, prepared on paper, is pricked out on the clay with an awl or some other sharp instrument. The paper is then peeled off and berries of some kind are then used to embolden the outline. Finally, the picture is filled in with pieces of bark, mosses, lichens and flower petals. The petals are applied so that they overlap in order to ensure that the rainwater runs off without harming the picture. Three out of four pictures have a religious theme and local clergy often bless the wells in their area. Some well-dressers regard their work as a sort of harvest festival offering. The work of 'dressing the wells' can take a week of hard labour, with many working through the night to get their dressing finished.

CYCLING

Long before the Tour de France was even thought of, James Moore from Bury St Edmunds won the world's first major cycling road race, held between Paris and Rouen in 1868.

Moore had to race in France because the authorities in England had outlawed cycling races on public roads on the grounds of safety.

DANGEROUS SPORTS CLUB

David Kirke, one of the founders of this very English Club (which was set up in the mid 1970's at Oxford University) invented modern bungee jumping in 1979 when he tied a rubber cord to his ankles and leapt from the Clifton Suspension Bridge in Bristol. He was arrested and fined £100. Other stunts devised and practised by Club members include:

1. Sliding down a black St. Moritz ski run in a rowing eight.
2. Hang gliding over active volcanoes off Kilimanjaro.

3. Buzzing the Eiffel tower in a microlight

4. Flying across the English Channel in the pouch of a helium-filled inflatable kangaroo.

5. Flying around Big Ben in a microlight while dressed in a gorilla suit.

6. Creating sculptures and riding them down ski runs.

7. Rolling down mountains inside giant plastic spheres (known as mountain zorbing).

8. Lying face down on a surfboard and hurtling down long flights of concrete steps (street luging).

9. Jumping down waterfalls without a raft or boat, protected only by a crash helmet and a life jacket.

10. Jumping from buildings, bridges and cliffs (Base jumping).

11. Being a human cannonball with a mediaeval trebuchet.

12. Flying through the air with the contraption used to launch fighter jets from aircraft carriers.

The club once held a cocktail party on Rockall, a jagged rock 200 miles out in the Atlantic. Members were however prevented from driving a double-decker London bus down a ski slope at St Moritz.

DICKENS, CHARLES (1812-1870)
A Dozen Facts

1. The great English novelist Charles Dickens was born at Landport, Portsea on 7 February 1812, to Elizabeth and John Dickens.

2. Charles Dickens's father, a clerk in the Navy Pay Office at Portsmouth dockyard, was transferred to London and then to the dockyard at Chatham in Kent. The young Dickens's years at Chatham were a very happy period in his life. But, sadly, Charles Dickens's happy childhood changed when his father was recalled to Somerset House, London. The nine-year-old Dickens was removed from a school he loved and the whole family moved to a rented two-storey terraced house in one of the poorest parts of Camden Town.

3. Two days after Charles Dickens's 12th birthday he was sent to work in a boot-blacking factory to bring in some money. At the blacking factory, in the Strand in London, he had to prepare pots of blacking for sale. This involved placing covers on the pots of paste-blacking, tying the covers with string and pasting printed labels onto the pots. 'No words can express the secret agony of my soul as I sunk into this companionship,' wrote Dickens much later. 'My early hope of growing up to be a learned and distinguished man crushed in my breast.'

4. Dickens worked at Warren's for 10 hours a day and shortly after he had started work there, his spendthrift father was arrested and sent to the Marshalsea debtors' prison.

5. On Charles Dickens's first visit to Marshalsea Prison his father told him to be warned by what he saw and to observe that if a man had twenty pounds a year, and spent nineteen pounds nineteen shillings and sixpence, he would be happy; but that a shilling spent the other way would make him wretched. His father's piece of advice was later immortalised in the novel *David Copperfield*. The character Mr Micawber in *David Copperfield* was largely based on Charles's father. Of all his work, *David Copperfield* is the closest portrayal of Charles Dickens's life.

6. It was the serial stories *The Pickwick Papers* (published by Chapman and Hall), which brought Charles Dickens the fame that he craved as a writer. The monthly serial started slowly (with only 400 copies of the first number being sold) but by the 15th number, the novel was selling a staggering 40,000 copies of each number. *The Pickwick Papers* was Charles Dickens's first novel. He was only 24-years-old.

7. Most of Charles Dickens's novels were originally published in a monthly serial format. Charles Dickens's major works include: *Sketches by Boz* (1836), *The Pickwick Papers* (1837), *Oliver Twist* (1838), *Nicholas Nickleby* (1839), *The Old Curiosity Shop* (1841), *Barnaby Rudge* (1841), *A Christmas Carol* (1843), *Martin Chuzzlewit* (1844), *Dombey and Son* (1848), *David Copperfield* (1850), *Bleak House* (1853), *Hard Times* (1854), *Little Dorrit* (1857), *A Tale of Two Cities* (1859), *Great Expectations* (1861), and *Our Mutual Friend* (1865).

8. It was not uncommon for Dickens to use people he knew as the basis for his characters. Paul Dombey Jr. in Dombey and Son was based on his disabled nephew, Henry Burnett, and the Character 'Tiny Tim' in Christmas Carol was originally called 'Tiny Fred' after his younger brother.

9. Charles Dickens's serialisations were like the soap operas of today, except he was the only scriptwriter. Many people, old and young, would look forward to the next episode of his latest story. Queen Victoria was one of his fans. No other author before him had reached a wider audience. Even those who weren't literate had the opportunity to enjoy his stories by attending public readings.

10. Dickens's colourful characters and his wonderful prose made him an exceptionally revered author. He was also very influential. Dickens's portrayal of the poor in his stories brought their plight to the public's attention. He altered people's attitudes to the impoverished and the downtrodden. Not only did he write about the poor in his fiction but he also helped the poor in real life through various charities and by spontaneously giving money to downtrodden people he came across in the street. Charles Dickens, along with a Miss Burdett-Coutts, even set up a home for fallen women in Shepherds Bush. He was a philanthropist who cared passionately about society's forgotten people. On top of all this he founded, ran, edited and often largely wrote a number of newspapers and magazines.

11. Throughout most of his life, Charles Dickens felt very strongly about the plight of the poor and the mistreatment of children. The mistreatment of pupils at Dotheboys Hall in *Nicholas Nickleby* was inspired by his visit in 1838 to several Yorkshire schools that were renowned for their brutality. The book *Nicholas Nickleby* led to the closure of several Yorkshire schools where pupils were being beaten and neglected. Dickens also advocated the abolition of slavery during his trip to America in 1842.

12. On June 1870, at the age of just 58, Charles Dickens died of a stroke, leaving *The Mystery of Edwin Drood* unfinished. The whole nation mourned his passing. He had, among other things, helped stamp out child labour, abolish cruel boarding schools,

and end public executions. No man in the world ever did more to improve the society in which he lived, or that which would follow. He was buried at Poet's Corner, Westminster Abbey. The inscription on his tombstone reads: 'He was a sympathiser to the poor, the suffering and the oppressed; and by his death, one of England's greatest writers is lost to the world'. Dickens wasn't just a great novelist; he was also one of the world's most potent and successful social reformers and campaigners.

DICKENS, CHARLES – QUOTATIONS FROM HIS NOVELS

1. 'One always begins to forgive a place as soon as it's left behind'. (*Little Dorrit*)

2. 'It is a melancholy truth that even great men have their poor relations'. (*Bleak House*)

3. 'Never be mean in anything. Never be false. Never be cruel. Avoid these three vices and I can always be hopeful of you.' (*David Copperfield*)

4. 'He'd make a lovely corpse.' (*Martin Chuzzlewit*)

5. 'He had but one eye, and the popular prejudice runs in favour of two'. (*Nicholas Nickleby*)

6. 'It was the best of times, it was the worst of times.' (*A Tale of Two Cities*)

7. 'We are so very 'umble.' (*David Copperfield*)

8. 'It is a far, far better thing that I do, than I have ever done; it is a far, far better rest that I go to, than I have ever known.' (*A Tale of Two Cities*)

9. 'Bah,' said Scrooge. 'Humbug!' (*A Christmas Carol*)

10. 'Annual income twenty pounds, annual expenditure nineteen nineteen six, result happiness. Annual income twenty pounds, annual expenditure twenty pounds nought and six, result misery.' (*David Copperfield*)

11. 'Please, sir, I want some more.' (*Oliver Twist*)

12. 'God bless us every one!' said Tiny Tim. (*A Christmas* Carol)

DOGS

The English are renowned for their love of animals, especially their pets. Here are a dozen English dog breeds:

1. Cavalier King Charles Spaniel
2. English Bulldog
3. English Cocker Spaniel
4. English Foxhound
5. English Setter
6. English Shepherd
7. Manchester Terrier
8. Norfolk Terrier
9. Old English Sheepdog
10. Staffordshire Bull Terrier
11. Sussex Spaniel
12. Yorkshire Terrier

DOCTORS

Two Dozen Great English Doctors

1. Addison, Thomas (1793-1860) – Discovered Addison's disease and did research on tuberculosis and pneumonia.
2. Anderson, Elizabeth Garrett (1836-1917) – First woman doctor in England.
3. Bacon, Roger (1214-1292) – Invented gunpowder, the magnifying glass and the telescope and published valuable works on mathematics and philosophy. Known as Doctor Mirabilis.

4. Blackwell, Elizabeth (1821-1910) – Born in England but the first woman doctor in the USA.

5. Bright, Richard (1789-1858) – Discovered Bright's disease, and much more.

6. Darwin, Charles (1809-1992) – Author of *The Origin of Species* and creator of the theory of evolution.

7. Darwin, Erasmus (1731-1802) – Grandfather of Charles Darwin and early thinker on evolution.

8. Grace, William Gilbert (1848-1915) – GP and greatest ever Test Cricketer.

9. Harvey, William (1578-1657) – Discovered circulation of the blood.

10. Heberden, William (1710-1801) – The first doctor to distinguish smallpox from chickenpox. Also first described angina pectoris.

11. Hodgkin, Thomas (1798-1866) – Described the glandular disease named after him.

12. Jenner, Edward (1749-1823) – Discoverer of vaccination

13. John of Gaddesden (1280-1361) – The model for Chaucer's *Doctor of Physic.*

14. Keats, John (1795-1821) – Better known as a poet than a medical man.

15. Linacre, Thomas (1460-1524) – Introduced licensing for doctors.

16. Lister, Joseph (1827-1912) – Father of antiseptic surgery.

17. Locke, John (1632-1704) – Doctor, scientist and philosopher.

18. Lower, Richard (1631-1691) – Early pioneer on work of pulmonary and cardiovascular anatomy and physiology.

19. Parkinson, James (1755-1824) – discoverer of Parkinson's disease. First doctor to recognise appendicitis.

20. Petty, William (1623-1687) – Inventor of modern economic theory.

21. Pott, Percival (1714-1788) – Gave his name to Pott's fracture and Pott's disease.

22. Roget, Peter Mark (1779-1869) – Author of the first thesaurus.

23. Snow, John (1813-1858) – First anaesthetist in the world and

epidemiologist who discovered that cholera is spread through contaminated water supplies.

24. Withering, William (1741-1799) – First doctor to connect dropsy to heart disease, and first man to introduce digitalis as a drug for heart disease.

DOVER: THE WHITE CLIFFS
Half a Dozen Facts

1. The white cliffs of Dover are among the most famous and symbolic of English landmarks. The white cliffs form part of the English coastline facing the Strait of Dover and France. For centuries the chalk cliffs of Dover have been a welcoming sight to many a returning sailor.

2. The famous white cliffs were brought to the forefront of many people's minds by the popular song 'There'll Be Bluebirds Over The White Cliffs of Dover' sung during the Second World War by forces' sweetheart, Dame Vera Lynn. Sadly, there are no bluebirds over, below or near to the White Cliffs of Dover because bluebirds are not found in England.

3. The soft, limestone cliffs were formed during the Cretaceous Period. The Cretaceous Period began from 144 to 65 million years ago. The cliffs are made up of billions of tiny fragments of marine animal shells.

4. On a clear day, the white cliffs are easily seen from the French coast.

5. Visitors are warned not to go too near the edge of the cliffs as large chunks have fallen off the edge of the cliffs and into the English Channel. On average, the constant movement of the sea eats away an inch from the base of the cliffs each year.

6. There are miles of hidden tunnels behind the cliff face. These were created during the Middle Ages. During the Napoleonic Wars, the tunnels were used to help defend England.

DRAKE, FRANCIS (1540-1596)

A Dozen Facts

1. He was a naval hero, England's best loved sea captain, but he was also a pirate.

2. Born in Devon, the son of a poor tenant farmer, he went to sea at the age of 13 and gained a reputation as an outstanding seaman.

3. In 1577, Drake was commissioned by Elizabeth I to lead an expedition to South America. He sailed down the West Coast of Africa, across the Atlantic, and down the coast of America and then, at the worst time of year, sailed through the newly discovered Straits of Magellan.

4. Drake sailed up the coast of South America, attacking one port after another. The inhabitants never suspected that an English vessel would reach such a distant point and their ships were unprepared and their ports were unprotected.

5. At Valparaiso, Drake took a big galleon which was stuffed with great wedges of pure gold. At Tarapaca he took a mass of silver, in bars, which had been brought down from the mines. At Arica he found more silver.

6. At Lima, Drake was told that a ship that had just sailed northwards, called the Cacafuego, was full of treasure. Drake chased after it, fired a shot through the mainmast and a hail of arrows onto the deck. He took possession of a vast treasure of gold, silver, rubies, emeralds and diamonds.

7. Having emptied the Cacafuego of treasure, Drake decided that he had damaged the Spanish sufficiently. He set the Cacafuego free. But the Spaniards were not about to let him go so easily. Three Spanish cruisers, fully armed, pursued Drake's single ship. Instead of running, Drake shortened sail to allow them to catch up with him. This so terrified the Spanish captains that all three of them turned and fled without firing a shot, swearing that they would not fight a captain who was so plainly not a man but a devil.

8. On getting back home, Drake and his crew became the first

men to sail around the world. Drake returned home laden with treasure. The voyage had taken three years and the Pelican had 'marked a furrow around the globe with her keel'.

9. Queen Elizabeth commanded that the Pelican (which was renamed the Golden Hind) be brought up the Thames. There the Queen went on board the most famous of all English ships and Francis Drake, adventurer and explorer, became Sir Francis Drake. He was also made mayor of Plymouth.

10. In 1587, when England was at war with Spain, Drake sailed into Cadiz harbour, setting fire to the ships of the Spanish fleet which were lying at anchor. It was an incident known as 'singeing the King of Spain's beard'.

11. In 1588, it was vice admiral Drake who interrupted his game of bowls on Plymouth Hoe to harass the Spanish Armada as it sailed up the Channel. Francis Drake was playing bowls at the time when he was told about the sighting of the Spanish Armada. He is reported to have said: 'There is plenty of time to win this game and thrash the Spaniards too'.

12. When the seemingly indestructible Drake finally died, succumbing to fever on a voyage to the West Indies, he was, of course, buried at sea.

DUNKING

Dunking a biscuit in a cup of tea is one of the great English pastimes. Some people think it rather 'common' but others just cannot enjoy a cup of tea without having a biscuit to dunk. The dunkers point out that at least one recent member of the Royal family was rumoured to be an enthusiastic dunker.

Whether you're a dunking fan or not, here is a list of half a dozen of the most popular biscuits to dunk into a cup of nice, hot tea:

1. Chocolate digestive biscuits
2. Rich Tea biscuits
3. Digestive biscuits

4. Ginger biscuits

5. Chocolate chip cookies

6. Bourbon biscuits

ECCENTRICS

A Dozen of the Oddest English Eccentrics

The people on this list are genuine, English eccentrics. They are not just people pretending to be eccentric by taking part in a charity event dressed as Elvis Presley. These are people who lived truly eccentric lives. They were unaware of their eccentricity and would not have described themselves as in any way strange.

Eccentricity is an essentially English phenomenon. It is, like so many things, something the English do infinitely better than anyone else. There are many who would like to be thought of eccentric and many who make every possible effort to appear eccentric. So, for example, exhibitionists, and those hoping to break into some branch of showbusiness, will frequently adopt some carefully thought-out form of dress or behaviour in order to draw attention to themselves. That is not eccentricity and they are not eccentrics. Nor are the individuals who dream up stunts to get themselves into the *Guinness Book of Records* 'eccentric'. Simply being frugal, living way beneath or beyond your means or choosing to live the life of a hermit may be odd but it isn't truly eccentric. Building a folly to provide employment for local workmen, or a focal point for visitors to admire, may be a trifle odd but it doesn't count as truly eccentric. Wearing flamboyant clothes (in the mode of Beau Brummel) or collecting vast quantities of something doesn't necessarily make an individual truly eccentric (though bibliomaniac Richard Heber makes it onto our list). We have not even included the composer Lord Berners on our list even though his behaviour has been widely described as eccentric. (He used the name Gerald Tyrwhitt when composing but later, when decomposing, reverted to Lord Berners.) Lord Berners hated company when on a train and in order to have the carriage to himself he used to check his temperature anally with a large thermometer every five minutes. This usually had the desired effect quite quickly. However, his behaviour had a clearly defined and understandable purpose and was carried out with precision and with purpose; it cannot, therefore, be properly described as 'eccentric'.

In our view, the real eccentric behaves in a way that seems to him to be entirely natural, logical and sensible. He doesn't do odd things occasionally. He doesn't sit in a bath of spaghetti to raise money for charity or push a bed up a mountain for a university rag day stunt. He doesn't simply wear flashy bow ties or dye his hair. He doesn't have an unusual hobby (restoring steam trains or dredging canals) because his whole life is unusual. The true eccentric's whole life is strange and he sees nothing odd in what he does or how he does it. His behaviour is, to him, perfectly rational. If he cared two hoots about how other people dressed or behaved (which he does not) then he would probably regard *them* as eccentric.

In other words the true eccentric, a breed of men and women with whom England has always been exceptionally well-endowed, never thinks of him or herself as eccentric at all.

Here is our list of the top dozen English eccentrics of all time. You will note that all of the people on our list are men. That is because most eccentrics have been men. There were (and are) many female eccentrics. But they weren't (and aren't) quite as eccentric as their male competitors. Eccentricity is simply something men do best. And you will note too that most of the people on our list are either rich or well-off. That is because when poor people behave in an eccentric way they are usually regarded as lunatics and locked up for their own protection. Sadly, only the wealthy can truly enjoy the delights of being genuinely eccentric. The wealthy can be eccentric in great style and (in the past, at least) their wealth frequently enabled them to ignore the law and escape the consequences.

1. John Mytton (1796-1834)
John Mytton's extraordinary adventures and eccentricities deserve a separate entry in this book. (See under Mytton, John.) If eccentrics were rated with little dog heads instead of rosettes (to give an idea of their 'barking' rating) then Mytton would have five little dog heads beside his name. His eccentricity took him right to the edge of madness. But he wasn't mad. He was just completely barking.

All other eccentrics must be measured against him. He was asked to leave Westminster School after a year for 'fighting with the masters'. He then went to Harrow where he lasted three days. When it was decided that he should attend Cambridge University he arranged for 2,000 bottles of port to be ready for his arrival. In the end he changed his mind and didn't go to Cambridge. There is no record of what happened to the port. When his creditors became a little too aggressive, Mytton moved to France. In a hotel in Calais he developed hiccups and decided to get rid of the problem by giving himself a fright. He set fire to his nightshirt. This cured the hiccups but he was badly burned. Advised to stay in bed for a month he arranged to go out for dinner. But when his dining companion sent a two horse equipage for him, Mytton, covered in bandages, refused to get into it, claiming that he would sooner walk than ride in a carriage with less than four horses. He walked a mile and a half.

2. Byron, George Gordon Noel, 6th Baron (1788-1824)

Famously described by one of his many mistresses as 'mad, bad and dangerous to know', Lord Byron was a poet and philanderer and is remembered as much for his life as for his work. He was a leading poet of the 19th century English Romantic movement and his poetry has been expertly described as irreverent, ironic, impudent, high-spirited, satirical, elegant, contemptuous, humorous, burlesque, unconventional, generous, humane and reckless. The same adjectives apply, equally accurately, to his life. Born with a deformed right foot which made him the butt of schoolboy jokes his mother had mood swings which made him distrust women in later life. His father had died when he was just three years old, but not before managing to spend Byron's mother's entire, considerable fortune. A female servant didn't help Byron's attitude towards women. She took a succession of male lovers with the nine year old Byron as a spectator. At the age of 10, he became the 6th baron and with the title he inherited considerable estates. He attended Harrow School and discovered homosexuality. His mother began an affair with a 23-year-old rake, Lord Grey de Ruthyn, who had made advances to the young Byron.

When he went to Cambridge in 1805, Byron patronised prostitutes with steadfast enthusiasm and fell in love with a choirboy called Edleston. When he put on weight he played cricket wearing six waistcoats so that he would sweat and lose weight. While at the university he published his first poems (*Hours of Idleness*) and took his first mistress, a girl called Caroline whom he dressed, and passed off as, a boy. The reviews of his first book were poor and so in 1809 he published *English Bards and Scotch Reviewers*, a satirical poem attacking the major literary figures of the time. He then left London and started a tour of Greece, Albania, Turkey and Spain with a friend called Hobhouse who was writing a book called *Sodomy Simplified* (which, surprisingly, never found a publisher). When Hobhouse abandoned him in Greece, Byron acquired a 15-year-old Greek boy called Nicolo and spent a good deal of money on prostitutes. He returned to England in 1812 and John Murray published *Childe Harold's Pilgrimage*. The poem, inspired by his journey, describes the exploits of a world-weary young lord who tries everything so young that he finds later life boring. Byron became an overnight celebrity. Young men imitated his brooding manner and his limp. Young women, attracted by his passion and his pleas for liberty and justice, threw themselves at him (though possibly not literally). Byron's new lovers included Lady Caroline Lamb and her mother-in-law Lady Melbourne.

When he returned to Cambridge, Byron began an incestuous affair with his half-sister Augusta. He was then seduced by a promiscuous woman called Lady Oxford. Byron and Augusta then moved to Newstead Abbey where she became pregnant. To silence the gossips, Byron, by now aged 26, married Lady Melbourne's niece, a prim heiress called Annabelle. The marriage wasn't much of a success, possibly because Byron continued to 'flirt' with his half sister and possibly because he was nearly always drunk. When his wife became pregnant he sodomised her late into her pregnancy. Exhausted by Byron's demands, by quarrels, by being constantly sodomised and by giving birth, Annabelle went home. When her parents found out what had been going on they would not let her return to the wicked lord. Suddenly the great poet was unfashionable and unwanted. Byron quit England in 1816. Having sold Newstead Abbey for £94,500 he rented a palazzo in Venice where he initiated orgies which shocked even the previously unshockable Venetians. Byron's home soon became pretty much a brothel. The man himself was now fat and balding though still in his early thirties. While in Italy he wrote *Don Juan*, a long, witty poem about a handsome young man's adventures with women. A tempestuous affair with a married woman caused some problems and Byron left Italy in rather a rush. He became an enthusiastic supporter of Italian and Greek freedom fighters and joined a secret Italian nationalist society. He was a freedom fighter in Greece, leading troops against the Turks, when he caught a fever and, in proper poetic fashion, died young at the age of 36. His family requested that he be buried in Westminster Abbey. Perhaps not entirely surprisingly, the request was refused.

3. Rev F. W. Densham (1870-1953)

When the Rev Densham was rector of the church in Warleggan, Cornwall he painted the 12th century church red and blue. The church pillars were painted with black and white stripes. This decor didn't go down too well with the congregation. In his final year as rector, the Rev Densham conducted most of his services in an empty church (on one occasion there was just one person attending a service, on all other occasions the rector was alone). But to keep him company the Rev Densham filled the church with cardboard cut-out figures and name cards and then delivered passionate sermons to his cardboard flock. Why didn't the parishioners go to church? Well, perhaps they were put off by the fact that if they turned up at all he would be incredibly rude to them. Or it might have been the fact that there was an eight-foot high barbed wire fence around the rectory. Or perhaps they were put off by the fact that the rectory was bare of furniture and that the rector lived on porridge and nettles. Saddest of all, behind the eight-foot high fence, the garden was full of roundabouts and other games which the rector had constructed for the local children. None ever visited and none ever used the toys he made.

4. William John Cavendish Bentinck Scott, 5th Duke of Portland (1800-1879)

The Duke was mad keen on building things. He built pagodas, lakes, a skating rink and a huge stable for a string of race horses which never raced (or were even ridden). He built the biggest indoor riding school in Europe. It was never used. He did, however, insist that all his staff learned to skate and skate regularly (whether they wanted to do or not). His most remarkable building was an underground ballroom which was 174ft long, and had a ceiling painted to represent a sunset. It was lit with a thousand gas lights. He built an underground railway to connect his house to the ballroom but never used the ballroom. He also had 15 miles of tunnel built under his estate so that he could move about without ever meeting anyone. An underground railway enabled staff to take meals the 150 yards from the kitchen to the dining room. One of the tunnels was big enough to take a coach and four. He loathed any sort of contact with people, and when he had to travel he did so in a specially built coach which had low seats and blinds. He would be driven to the nearest station and the coach would be put onto a special flat car at the back of the train. As well as the underground ballroom he also built an underground billiard room, big enough for 12 full-sized tables, and several underground libraries. Like the ballroom, these remained unused. All the underground rooms were painted pink. Many, like the rooms in the main house, had a plumbed-in lavatory right in the middle of the room. At one point the Duke employed 15,000 workmen. Every one of them was given a donkey and an umbrella as a bonus and no one was ever sacked unless they acknowledged the Duke's presence. Anyone who spoke to him, nodded, bowed, touched their cap or glanced in his direction would be fired on the spot. The Duke wrote to his staff if he wanted to tell them to do something. He hated human contact so much that if he needed the doctor he would make the physician wait outside the bedroom door and shout details of his symptoms through the door. He had a vast collection of wigs, false beards and false moustaches so that if he had to go out into the world he could do so without being recognised. However, since very few people knew what he looked like this was probably unnecessary. The uke gave away vast amounts of money to local charities and to poor families and despite his eccentricities was much loved.

5. George Hanger, later Baron Coleraine (1751-1824)
By the age of 22, George had married a gypsy, fought three duels, reached the rank of colonel and been wounded in the American War of Independence. He then retired to devote himself to gambling,

drinking, racing and whoring. He wasn't terribly good as a gambler. He once bet £500 that 20 turkeys would beat 20 geese over a 10-mile racecourse. He lost. He spent 18 months in a debtors' prison and when he came out he went into business as a coal merchant.

6. Edward Wortley Montagu (1713-1776)

Montagu spent most of his life roaming around the Middle East dressed in Turkish costume, but his eccentric life started early. He ran away from Westminster School and exchanged places with a young sweep so that his disappearance wouldn't be noticed. After working as a chimney boy he apprenticed himself to a fisherman and sold flounders in Rotherhithe. At the age of 13 he enrolled himself at Oxford University as a student of Oriental languages. He immediately seduced his landlady. He then dressed as a cabin boy and went to Portugal on board a merchant ship. In Portugal he became a mule driver. When eventually brought home his parents sent him to the West Indies with a tutor. Montagu returned to London at the age of 17 and married a washerwoman. She was the first of many wives. He subsequently acquired additional wives in Egypt, Italy, Spain and elsewhere and his other conquests included an Egyptian serving girl. In between marriage ceremonies he became an army officer, a scholar in Oriental languages and MP for Huntingdon. In London he wore an iron wig studded with diamonds (he changed the diamonds every day) and collected snuffboxes and debts. He had acquired another wife while visiting a highwayman in prison and with accusations of bigamy over his head he left the country again. At his first port of call, Alexandria, he met and eloped with the wife of the Danish consul, after falsely telling the woman that her husband had been drowned at sea. He wandered around the Middle East (papers relating his travels were read out at meetings of the Royal Society), put the Danish consul's wife into a nunnery and wandered off. He went back for her several years later (she was faithfully waiting for him) and married her. Things weren't perfect, however, and so Montagu changed his religion from Catholic to Moslem and married his black Egyptian serving girl. He ended up in Venice attended by a black African servant and two half-naked eunuchs. He lived in a Venetian palazzo and flew the Turkish flag on his gondola. At this point his father died, and Montagu discovered that in order to benefit financially he had to marry and have a son. So he put an advertisement in the London papers inviting genteel and pregnant women to apply to be his wife. Sadly, before he could travel back to London to select the winner (from a number of applicants) he died after a bone got stuck in his throat.

7. Richard Heber, (1774-1833)

Heber was born in Cheshire and by the time he was eight years old he had a sizeable library of own, all properly catalogued. After his father died and he inherited the family fortune he started collecting in earnest. He invariably bought three copies of any book he liked (one to store, one to read and one to lend) and filled two London houses, a house in Cheshire and houses in Paris, Brussels, Antwerp and Ghent with books. He would travel miles to buy a single book and in Paris he once bought an entire library of 30,000 volumes in one go. In all his houses the rooms, cupboards, passageways and corridors were choked with books.

8. George Osbaldeston (1786-1866)

George reckoned that any week in which he didn't spend six days in the saddle was a week wasted. His feats of sporting endurance are legendary. He once won a bet by galloping 200 miles in under nine hours (he used 27 horses for the ride). At a ball in Lincoln he noticed one attractive woman admiring the orchid worn by another. The orchid wearer rudely snubbed the admiring woman and Osbaldeston was incensed. He leapt onto his horse and rode to a private conservatory 25 miles away where he bought the best orchid available. After four hours of hard riding he reappeared in the ballroom and presented the orchid to the snubbed woman. They reputedly danced until dawn though what happened then is not recorded.

9. Simon Ellerton (1695-1799)

Ellerton was a keen walker who often walked from Durham (where he lived) to London. He would happily do the journey to perform errands for the local gentry. While out walking one day he picked up a stone for a cottage he was building. This soon became a habit and before long he had become accustomed to picking up one or two stones every time he went out. He would put them on his head to carry them, initially claiming that he could walk more comfortably with a weight on his head than he could without. He carried on with this even after his cottage had been completed. Until his death he always carried a heavy stone on his head when he left home. When asked why, he would, in later life, explain that the stone was there to keep his hat on.

10. Thomas Gibson Bowles (known as Cap'en Tommy) – (1842-1922)
Bowles was the founder and publisher of the magazines the *Lady* and *Vanity Fair*. When his wife died leaving him with four children under the age of 10 he decided to have his daughters clothed by the naval tailor who made clothes for his sons. As a result, his two daughters, Sydney and Dorothy, wore thick blue serge naval uniforms and sailors' caps until they were 17. (Sydney would later become Lady Redesdale, the mother of the famous Mitford girls.) When the girls eventually managed to persuade their father that they should be dressed as young women, Bowles consulted an 'actress' friend. With her guidance the girls were dressed in low-necked black velvet gowns with red sashes. Bowles was MP for King's Lynn from 1892 to 1906 and in 1899 he announced to his daughter Dorothy, by then keeping home for him, that he was fed up with politics and intended to move to China. He told Dorothy to close up the house and pack. She did as she was told. All the furniture was covered in dust-sheets and a caretaker hired to look after the house. Dorothy then sat outside the house, with the luggage, in a four-wheeled carriage waiting for her father to join her. But as Bowles left the house it started to rain. He leant into the cab and said: 'My dear child, it's raining. We won't go.'

11. Sir Thomas Barrett-Lennard (1857 to 1918)
Sir Thomas, the squire of Belhus in Essex, was a great animal lover. On muddy days, if he thought the going was too heavy for a horse to pull his carriage with him inside it, he would jump out and run alongside to save the horse the effort. He loved all animals; his servants were instructed to keep a fresh bowl of water in the corn rick for the rats, and, on one occasion, when he saw a butcher mistreating a pony he tore off his coat and thrashed the man. He cared about humans too. He would often answer his own front door to save his

butler the trouble and dressed so scruffily that he was once given a tip for opening his park gates to a visiting carriage.

12. Francis Henry Egerton, eighth Earl of Bridgewater (1756- 1829)

The Earl loved his dogs and treated them like dinner guests. With an annual income of £40,000 a year he could afford to do pretty much what he liked. At dinner the dogs sat on chairs dressed in fashionable finery. They had handmade leather shoes on their feet and linen napkins round their necks. A footman stood behind each dog. If a dog didn't behave properly it would suffer the indignity of being dressed in yellow servants' livery and sent to eat in the servants' hall for a week. When the dogs were taken for a walk, a servant with an umbrella would accompany them to make sure they didn't get wet. Lord Bridgewater also had a passion for boots. He wore a different pair each day, never wearing the same boots twice and so never having the joy of wearing a comfortable pair. Each night the boots he had taken off would be placed alongside the previous day's boots and by the time he died, the house was filled with rows and rows of them. They were not cleaned so that he could find out what the weather had been like simply by finding the boots for that day. His boots were his diary. Egerton lived in France for 30 years but never learned French. In later years he used to entertain guests by ordering his secretary to read them extracts from a long and constantly changing will. In the gardens of his Paris home he kept 300 rabbits, 300 pigeons and 300 partridges. The birds had their wings clipped. This menagerie enabled him to wander into his garden and shoot his dinner when the fancy took him. When he travelled he did not do so lightly. Packing would take months. On one occasion he set off followed by sixteen carriages laden with luggage. He returned hours after setting off having abandoned his trip after an unsatisfactory lunch at an inn. When he died, each servant received a mourning suit, a cocked hat and three pairs of worsted stockings. A monument on his grave depicts a woman with a stork behind her, an elephant by her side and a dolphin at her feet. Needless to say Egerton designed the monument himself.

ELECTRIC LIGHT

In 1860, Joseph Swan (1828-1914), an English chemist and physicist who was born in Sunderland, produced, and patented, the first electric lightbulb. He had begun working on his lightbulb in 1850, using carbonised paper filaments in a glass bulb. Swan's house was the first in the world to be lit by an incandescent electric light bulb. When Swan visited the Paris Exhibition in 1881, the whole city was lit with electric light, thanks to his invention, and there were exhibits of his inventions. (Thomas Edison, in America, was just getting round to developing his first light bulb at this time.) In 1878, Swan received another patent for a much improved electric light bulb which had a better vacuum and a carbonised thread as a filament. Edison obtained patents in America for a copy of the Swan lightbulb and dishonestly ran an advertising campaign claiming that the invention was his own.

ELIZABETH I (1533-1603)

When Queen Elizabeth sat on the throne of England in 1558, her country was in ruin and virtually bankrupt. England was despised abroad and confused at home.

In 1603, when she died, it was the end of an era of heroes. It was, for England, a golden time. Elizabeth was the most outstanding queen the world has ever seen. Only Queen Victoria comes close.

Here are two dozen facts about Queen Elizabeth I:

1. Elizabeth, Queen of England and Ireland, and the fifth and last monarch of the Tudor dynasty, was born on 7 September 1533 at Greenwich Palace, Kent, to King Henry VIII and his second wife, Anne Boleyn. It was confidently predicted by physicians and astrologers that King Henry and Anne Boleyn would have a boy and so when Elizabeth was born there was much disappointment all round. King Henry now had two legitimate children, the 17-year-old Princess Mary Tudor by his first wife, Catherine of Aragon, and the red-haired Princess Elizabeth. But both were girls.

2. Less than six months after her birth, Elizabeth went to live in Hatfield, north of London. It was the custom in Tudor times for children of royalty to live in separate households from their parents.

3. In 1534, Henry VIII managed to persuade Parliament to pass a new Act of Succession that allowed Elizabeth, and any more children her mother should have, to be the only legitimate heirs to the throne. Mary Tudor, who was still only a teenager, was thus declared illegitimate and demoted from princess to lady-in-waiting to her half sister, Elizabeth. Mary Tudor was also banished from ever seeing her mother again.

4. Wanting a reason that would free him of his wife because he had grown to despise her, and believed that his marriage to her was cursed because she had failed to produce a male heir, King Henry VIII had Protestant Queen Anne Boleyn beheaded at the Tower of London on 19th May 1536 for alleged multiple adultery and for incest with her own brother. No doubt King Henry's determination to dispose of his wife was strengthened even further when he fell in love with the rather retiring Jane Seymour.

5. Elizabeth was not yet three years of age when her mother was executed.

6. A few days before Anne Boleyn's beheading in 1536, Elizabeth, like her half sister Mary Tudor before her, was declared illegitimate and excluded from the line of succession. King Henry VIII married Jane Seymour less than a fortnight after Anne's execution. Ironically, just as Anne Boleyn was Catherine of Aragon's maid of honour, so Jane Seymour was Anne Boleyn's maid of honour.

7. On the 12 October 1537, King Henry finally had his much-awaited son, Edward VI, with his third wife, Jane Seymour. Since his half sisters had been decreed illegitimate, Edward VI was now first in line to the throne. Sadly, Jane Seymour died less than a fortnight after the birth of her son.

8. Elizabeth, who was brought up in the Protestant faith, was a natural scholar and loved to study. Elizabeth was very well educated and learnt a number of languages. She could speak

French fluently by the time she was 14 and also learnt Italian, Latin, Greek, Flemish and Spanish. Elizabeth also knew some Welsh. She was also a competent horsewoman with a love of riding at great speeds. In addition, Elizabeth could dance, compose music and play the lyre, lute and virginals skilfully.

9. In 1544, King Henry VIII's third Act of Succession reinstated Elizabeth and her half sister Mary to the line of the throne although it did not officially recognise them as legitimate. Their half brother, Prince Edward VI (by King Henry and his third wife, Jane Seymour) was still first in line to the throne, Mary Tudor was second in line and Elizabeth was third in line to the throne.

10. On 29 January 1547, Henry VIII died after a short illness and, as requested when he was alive, was buried next to his third wife, Jane Seymour. Elizabeth was residing at Enfield when she learnt of her father's death. Although she had never shared a close relationship with her father, Elizabeth did admire and respect him. Throughout her life, Elizabeth would often proudly refer to herself in public as the daughter of King Henry VIII.

11. On Henry VIII's death, Elizabeth's half-brother, Edward VI, became King but because he was only nine years old his uncle, Edward Seymour, was appointed Lord Protector and head of the Council of Regency. Edward VI became the first Protestant to sit on the English throne.

12. After her father's death, Elizabeth lived for a while with her stepmother Catherine Parr (Henry VIII's last wife) at Chelsea Palace. By the end of 1548, the 15-year-old Elizabeth had acquired a household of her own.

13. In 1550, the Earl of Warwick (who named himself the Duke of Northumberland in 1551) assumed power of the regency after masterminding the fall of Edward Seymour.

14. On July 6, 1553, King Edward VI died, probably from tuberculosis. Worried about losing his powerful position, Edward's Chief Minister, the now Duke of Northumberland, had managed to persuade the devout Protestant King to contravene the 1544 Act of Succession, to exclude his half-sisters from the succession and to make the Duke's daughter-in-law (also the King's cousin), Lady Jane Grey, as the next heir to the

throne. The unwilling Lady Jane was proclaimed Queen on 10 July. Mary was furious, and raised an army to fight for the crown. Lady Jane very happily relinquished the crown when ordered to do so, and the 37-year-old Catholic Mary Tudor was proclaimed Queen on 19 July. Lady Jane and her husband, Guildford Dudley were sentenced to death at the Tower of London. The tragic, sweet teenager Lady Jane Grey became known as the 'Nine-Day Queen'.

15. As Queen, devout Roman Catholic Mary Tudor overturned the anti-Catholic laws that had been introduced by her father, King Henry VIII. And she went to great lengths to restore Catholicism into England. Her persecution of Protestant rebels, and the execution of hundreds of heretics, earned her the nickname, 'Bloody Mary'.

16. On 18 March 1554, Elizabeth was taken to the Tower of London on the orders of her half sister, Queen Mary. The exceedingly unpopular Queen Mary believed her very popular half-sister to be involved in a plot with Sir Thomas Wyatt to overthrow her. Despite Elizabeth's pleas to her half-sister claiming her innocence, she was still sent to the Tower. Thomas Wyatt gave a speech minutes before he was executed, exonerating Elizabeth from all complicity in the rebellion. That speech helped gain Elizabeth her release and in the May of 1554, Elizabeth was freed from the Tower of London after two months imprisonment. She was sent to the royal palace at Woodstock in Oxfordshire under house arrest. It was with the help of Queen Mary's new husband Philip II of Spain (who became King of Spain in 1556), that Elizabeth was finally freed from house arrest and allowed to return to Hatfield. In November 1558, Queen Mary knew that she didn't have much longer to live and, with the encouragement of Philip of Spain, wrote to her half-sister, Elizabeth, telling her that she would allow her to succeed the throne only if she agreed to certain conditions. One of the conditions was that she would retain the Roman Catholic faith in England.

17. Whilst in the grounds of Hatfield House, 25-year-old Elizabeth learnt the news of her half-sister's death and was informed that she was now Queen of England. On learning of her accession,

she quoted in Latin from the 118th Psalm: 'This is the Lord's doing; it is marvellous in our eyes.'

18. In 1559, shortly after Elizabeth came to the throne, Mary Tudor's Catholic legislation was repealed, and Elizabeth became Supreme Governor (and not Supreme Head as her father had been) of the Church of England. She helped to restore England to Protestantism.

19. After Elizabeth nearly died from smallpox in 1562, Parliament worried that civil war would erupt upon her death if she did not produce an heir to the throne. MPs urged her to marry, as did her advisers. The pressure was increased by the fact that nobody believed that a woman could rule by herself.

20. Elizabeth was seen as the best catch in the whole of Europe. With her red hair and pale skin, Queen Elizabeth was striking in appearance. She enjoyed wearing the latest fashions (owning over 2,000 dresses) and adorned herself ostentatiously with expensive jewels. She was a hugely popular queen and would often go on walkabout tours and talk to the young, the old, the rich and the poor alike. She was a Queen who was wedded to the English people, and the people loved her for it. They called her Good Queen Bess. Queen Elizabeth had many suitors competing for her hand in marriage, including Philip II of Spain who had been married to her half-sister, Mary Tudor. At one point, marriage negotiations were seriously planned to François the Duke of Anjou (youngest son of Henry II and Catherine de'Medici) whom she nicknamed her 'frog'. Although she had serious romances with several lovers during her reign, Queen Elizabeth I never married. She was, however, something of a flirt. It is possible that Elizabeth deliberately didn't marry so that she could use the possibility of marriage as a diplomatic tool. Elizabeth's life as a spinster earned her the nickname, the 'Virgin Queen', a nickname which she herself promoted.

21. Over the early years of her reign, Elizabeth had dramatically improved her country's financial position through the efforts of officially approved pirates. Sir Francis Drake, for example, had enriched the nation considerably when he had been commissioned by the Queen as a privateer ('privateer' was

Elizabeth's politically correct name for 'pirate'). Drake's raids against Spanish colonies had proved very lucrative.

22. Before the defeat of the Spanish Armada, which was won by a combination of violent storms, well-built ships and the brilliant tactics of the English fleet, Queen Elizabeth gave a now legendary speech to her troops at Tilbury as they awaited the arrival of the Spanish Armada in 1588. This patriotic speech endeared her to the people of England. The defeat of the Spanish Armada firmly established England as the world's leading naval power and increased Queen Elizabeth's popularity ten-fold. The defeat of the Spanish Armada proved to all those who were sceptical that a woman was just as capable as any man as a war time leader.

23. In 1599, Elizabeth sent the 2nd Earl of Essex to Ireland to defeat Catholic Irish rebels who were rebelling against the anti-Catholic laws that Elizabeth had imposed. Essex fell out of favour with Elizabeth when he made an unauthorised treaty with the Irish and returned to England without the Queen's consent. This led Elizabeth to dismiss him from all his offices and stop most of his income. As revenge, and encouraged by rebels, he tried to get the people of London to revolt against Elizabeth. In 1601, the Earl was executed for leading a rebellion against Elizabeth's government. The English courtier and soldier had been a favourite of Queen Elizabeth's, even though she had shared a rather tempestuous relationship with him.

24. On 24 March 1603, aged 69, Queen Elizabeth, the last of the Tudor Monarchs, died at Richmond Palace, Surrey. Her reign had lasted for nearly 45 years. Elizabeth was buried at Westminster Abbey.

Queen Elizabeth reigned during a time when women were considered far from equal to men, but she was one of England's greatest sovereigns. She helped unify the country against foreign enemies and led the country to victory over the Spanish. She was a proud, strong-willed, quick-witted and a highly intelligent woman who was a shrewd judge of character. She was determined, cautious and secretive, and kept her thoughts and feelings close to her heart, which always kept even those around her guessing.

Elizabeth's reign was a time of great expansion and discovery. The adventurer, Sir Walter Ralegh named an American state 'Virginia' in the Queen's honour. And Sir Francis Drake became the first Englishman to circumnavigate the world. It was also a time of great poets and playwrights (most notably William Shakespeare, Ben Jonson and Christopher Marlowe).

By the end of Elizabeth's reign, however, the nation was not in a good state. Continuing troubles in Ireland, poor harvests, rising prices and increasing poverty had caused a huge dent in Elizabeth's popularity. Nevertheless, the shortcomings of her successor, King James I, soon restored Elizabeth's reputation with the people as one of England's greatest rulers. They didn't like him, and missed her.

Elizabeth's 45-year reign is considered to be England's 'Golden Age'. She had many faults: she was unscrupulous and often ready to lie if she thought it would be to her advantage; she was vain and easily influenced by flatterers; and she was rarely grateful to those around her. But she cared passionately for England and the English. She worked hard to govern wisely and well. And she has been described as the 'bravest woman who ever lived'. When she first addressed Parliament she said: 'Nothing, nothing, no worldly thing under the sun is so dear to me as the love and goodwill of my subjects.' During her life she proved that she meant it.

ELIZABETH I'S SPEECH AT TILBURY

Queen Elizabeth gave a legendary speech to her troops at Tilbury as they awaited the arrival of the Spanish Armada in 1588.

Here is an extract from it:

'My loving people, we have been persuaded by some that are careful of our safety to take heed how we commit ourselves to armed multitudes for fear of treachery, but I assure you I do not desire to live to distrust my faithful and loving people. Let tyrants fear; I have always so behaved myself under God, I have placed my chiefest strength and safeguard in the loyal hearts and goodwill of my subjects. And therefore I am come amongst you, as you see, at this time not for my recreation and disport, but being resolved in the midst and heat of battle to live and die amongst you all. To lay down for God, my kingdom and for my people, my honour and my blood even in the dust. I know I have the body of a weak and feeble woman, but I have the heart and stomach of a King and a King of England too and think it foul scorn that Parma or Spain or any Prince of Europe should dare to invade the borders of my realm; to which, rather than any dishonour shall grow by me, I myself will take up arms, I myself will be your General, Judge and Rewarder of every one of your virtues in the field. I know already for your forwardness you have deserved rewards and crowns; and we do assure you, on the word of a Prince, they shall be duly paid you.'

ELIZABETH II
A Dozen Facts

1. Queen Elizabeth II of England was born on April 21st 1926 at 17 Bruton Street, London. Her birthday is officially celebrated in June. The Queen was christened Elizabeth Alexandra Mary. Her Majesty was named Elizabeth after her mother; Alexandra after her great-grandmother; and Mary after her grandmother, Queen Mary. In appearance, the Queen is said to look very much like her grandmother, Queen Mary. When she was born, Princess Elizabeth was third in line to the crown. She became Queen on her father's death in 1952. The Princess was having a break in a tree-house in a remote part of Kenya at the time when she learnt that her father, King George VI had died. The Queen was 25-years-old, the same age that Elizabeth I was when she came to the throne. Her coronation took place in Westminster Abbey on 2 June 1953.

2. In addition to being Head of State, the Queen's other senior positions include Supreme Governor of the Church of England, Head of the Armed Forces and Head of the Commonwealth.

3. The Queen made her first public speech at the age of 14. She made a three-minute recording for the BBC *Children's Hour* programme to help raise the morale of the thousands of children who had been evacuated during World War II.

4. The Queen is the only person in Britain who is allowed to drive without numberplates on her motor car.

5. The Queen's full official title is 'Elizabeth the Second, by the Grace of God, of the United Kingdom of Great Britain and Northern Ireland and of Her other Realms and Territories Queen, Head of the Commonwealth, Defender of the Faith'.

6. Renowned for her love of corgi dogs, the Queen owned her first corgi, named Susan, on her 18th birthday. It is said that the Queen even took Susan with her on her honeymoon. A new breed of dog was introduced called the 'dorgi' after one of the Queen's corgis mated with Princess Margaret's dachshund, Pipkin.

7. The Queen is very fond of, and knowledgeable about, horse racing and horse breeding. The Queen received her first pony at the age of four. The pony, called Peggy, was given to her by her grandfather, King George V. The Queen also enjoys racing pigeons and is Patron of the Royal Pigeon Racing Association.

8. The Queen and her cousin, the Duke of Edinburgh, were married in Westminster Abbey on 20 November 1947. Their wedding cake was made by McVitie and Price Ltd. Owing to the fact that post-war rationing was still in place, the ingredients for the wedding cake were given by Australian Girl Guides as a wedding gift. The wedding cake was a staggering 9ft high. The Queen's wedding ring is made from a nugget of Welsh gold from the Clogau St David's mine near Dolgellau. Together, the Queen and the Duke of Edinburgh have four children: Prince Charles (1948), Princess Anne (1950), Prince Andrew (1960), and Prince Edward (1964).

9. The Queen and the Duke of Edinburgh are great-great-grandchildren of Queen Victoria. The Duke of Edinburgh is a direct descendent of Queen Victoria's third child, Alice. And the Queen is a direct descendent of Queen Victoria's eldest child, Prince Albert Edward.

10. The only time Queen Elizabeth failed to give a Christmas broadcast during her reign was in 1969 when a repeat of the film the *Royal Family* was shown.

11. Every evening at seven o'clock the Queen receives a red box filled with documents (including an account of the day in Parliament, Foreign Office telegrams, weekly summaries of her 15 other realms sent by the Governors-General, etc.). She is expected to read all these documents by the following morning.

12. The Queen is patron of over 600 charities and organisations.

ENGLISHMEN

A Dozen of the Greatest

1. Isaac Newton
2. Charles Darwin
3. Charles Dickens
4. Oliver Cromwell
5. William Shakespeare
6. Thomas Malthus
7. Winston Churchill
8. Francis Bacon
9. Michael Faraday
10. Charles Babbage
11. Joseph Lister
12. Alfred the Great

ENGLISHWOMEN

A Dozen of the Greatest

1. Queen Elizabeth I
2. Queen Victoria
3. Boudicca

4. Elizabeth Fry

5. Aphra Behn

6. Edith Cavell

7. Mrs Beeton

8. Jane Austen

9. Emily Brontë

10. Charlotte Brontë

11. Margaret Thatcher

12. Mary Wollstonecraft

Note: Florence Nightingale was born in Italy.

FIRSTS

A List of Two Dozen of England's Firsts

1. On 1st November 1848, the first railway station bookstall was opened at Euston by W.H. Smith.

2. In 1853, the first pillar box in England was erected at Botchergate, Carlisle.

3. In 1880, Her Majesty's Theatre in Carlisle was the first theatre in England to have electricity.

4. In 1928, the first county in England to try out tarmacadam on its roads was Kent.

5. The poet, Alexander Pope, planted in his garden the first weeping willow tree in England. All the weeping willows in England are descended from that one tree.

6. In 1721, John Lombe opened the first silk mill in Derby, England, making Derby one of the first English towns to be industrialised in the 18th century.

7. The first tour operator, Thomas Cook, arranged his first package tour in 1841. The tour was a train journey to a meeting in Loughborough on the newly opened Midland railway line from Leicester. The fare, which included lunch, was a shilling per head.

8. Around 1600, Francis Godwin, Bishop of Hereford, wrote the first science fiction story in the English language. The book, which was published after his death in 1633, was called *The Man in the Moon*.

9. Aphra Behn, who was born in 1640, was England's first female novelist and playwright.

10. In 1794, William Murdock invented a way to light his house by gas, enabling him to be the first person in the world to have his house lit that way. His house was in Redruth, Cornwall.

11. Causey Arch – built in 1726 – in Durham was the world's first railway bridge.

12. The first public street in England to be lit with gas was Pall Mall, London. The gas lamps on Pall Mall were lit on January 28 1807.

13. On 2 February 1852, the first water-flushed toilet for men was opened in Fleet Street, London. The first women's flushed toilet was opened on 11 February in Bedford Street, London.

14. The year 1843 saw the first Christmas card in England.

15. The first person to walk across Grosvenor Bridge in Chester, when it opened in 1832, was Queen Victoria, who was just 13 years old at the time and still a Princess.

16. In 1825, in Colnbrook in Aylesbury, Buckinghamshire, Richard Cox produced the first Cox's orange pippin apple.

17. The first one pound notes were issued in 1797. They were replaced by one pound coins in 1988.

18. In 1860, Joseph Malin opened the first fish and chip shop in London.

19. The first golf club at St Andrews was founded in 1784.

20. In 1836, the first train ran from London Bridge to Greenwich.

21. In 1622, the first English newspaper appeared called *Weekly News*.

22. Lord Byron's daughter, Ada, Countess of Lovelace was England's (and the world's) first computer programmer. The modern programming language ADA is named after the countess.

23. On September 22 1955, the first advertisement was shown on television. The advertisement was for Gibbs S R Toothpaste.

24. On November 8th 1920 Rupert Bear was born – making his first ever appearance on the cartoon page in the *Daily Express*.

FISH AND CHIPS

There really is nothing more English than fish and chips. The English are known almost everywhere in the world for their fish and chip shops, and one of the things tourists from abroad like to sample when in England is 'fish and chips'.

For a long time, fish and chips were never sold together but were sold in separate shops. It was in 1860 that Joseph Malin combined the two and opened the first fish and chip shop in London's East End.

FOLLIES
England's Dozen Most Magnificent Follies

Follies were very fashionable in England during the 18th and early 19th century, especially amongst the wealthy. A folly is defined as: 'an eccentric, generally nonfunctional (and often deliberately unfinished) structure erected to enhance a romantic landscape'.

1. The Gothic Temple, Stowe, Buckinghamshire
Designed in the mid 18th century by James Gibbs. The gothic temple, built of ironstone from Northamptonshire, is dedicated to the 'Liberties of our Ancestors'. The temple is considered to be the most beautiful building in the gardens at Stowe.

2. The Temple of the Four Winds, Castle Howard, North Yorkshire
Designed by Sir John Vanbrugh at the start of the 18th century. Sadly, Sir John Vanbrugh, who also helped build the house and buildings on the estate, did not live long enough to see the completion of the Temple of the Winds.

3. The Triangular Lodge, Rushton, Northamptonshire
Built in the late 16th century by Catholic politician Sir Thomas Tresham, who was once imprisoned for 15 years for his Catholic faith. During his time in prison, Sir Thomas Tresham became obsessed with the Holy Trinity and, as soon as he was released, built the Triangular Lodge. This magnificent building symbolises the 'three' of the Holy Trinity in every part of its construction. The Triangular Lodge is thought to be the earliest true folly.

4. The Temple of Apollo, Stourhead, Wiltshire
Architect Henry Flitcroft designed the Temple of Apollo in 1765. He also designed the Temple of Flora, the Pantheon and Alfred's Tower for the spectacular gardens that are now in the care of the National Trust.

5. The Great Pagoda, Kew Gardens, London
In 1761, Sir William Chambers built the 163ft high pagoda for the Dowager Princess of Wales, Augusta. The narrowness of the stairs means that the Pagoda is not open to the public. However, one can admire the numerous other buildings built by Sir William at Kew Gardens.

6. Sham Castle, Wimpole Park, Cambridgeshire
Sanderson Miller was commissioned by the First Earl of Hardwicke to build a replica of the sham castle at Hagley on his Wimpole estate. Unfortunately, years of delay in the building meant that the First Earl of Hardwicke did not live to see the completion of Sham Castle, which was built around 1772. Since the folly was not even seen by the person who ordered it to be built, the Sham Castle is possibly the truest folly on our list.

7. Ralph Allen's Sham Castle, Bath, Somerset
This sham castle is set in a commanding position, and can be seen from miles around. It was built in 1762 by Sanderson Miller for Ralph Allen, and is made of local stone.

8. Lord Berner's Folly, Farringdon, Oxfordshire
Built in 1935, and said to be the last true folly to be constructed. The largely square tower is 140ft high.

9. The Red House, Painswick Rococo Garden, Gloucestershire House

One of several architectural designs at Rococo Garden, and is a popular venue for wedding ceremonies. The asymmetrical Red House was built in the mid 18th century.

10. Folly Arch, Brookmans Park, Hertfordshire

Built in the mid 18th century by Sir Jeremy Sambrooke. The arch, which is built entirely of bricks, is said to contain a farthing between each pair of bricks.

11. The Spectacle, Boughton Park, Northamptonshire

Constructed in 1770 by William Wentworth, 2nd Earl of Stratfford. The Spectacle – one of seven follies at the park – has two identical castle-like towers that are joined together by an arch.

12. Old John Folly, Bradgate Park, Newtown Linford, Leicestershire

This folly sits on the highest hill in the park. Old John Folly is a two-storey castellated tower with a stone arch attached to the side of it, giving the impression of a beer mug (especially if seen in semi-darkness). The folly was built as a memorial to an estate worker (and beer lover) called John who was tragically killed when a flagpole landed on him during the celebrations of the Earl of Stamford's son's 21st birthday.

GAMES

The English invented all the world's most popular sports. But they also invented many unusual games too. Here's a short list of just a few of the oddest:

1. Marbles

There is, surprisingly, a season for the game of marbles (a sport in which contestants flick their own small, glass balls at those of their opponent). The marbles themselves are often very prettily coloured. Since around 1600 an annual marbles contest has taken place at Tinsley Green in Sussex. The game was originally a contest between two men fighting for the hand of a beautiful local girl. (There is no record of what she thought of this method of deciding her fate.) Today teams of six players compete in a circular concrete rink which is six feet in diameter. Forty nine marbles are placed in the centre of the rink and each player in turn flicks a marble from his index finger, using his thumb. The aim is to knock as many marbles as possible out of the rink but to leave the flicked marble inside the rink. A successful player shoots again. An unsuccessful player has to leave his marble alongside the 49 which were in the rink at the start. Eventually, a winner is found.

2. Conkers

The game of conkers gets its name from the word 'conquerors'. The word 'conkers' is a cockney vulgarism which crept in during the early part of the 20th century. The game, which is played with the fruit of the horse chestnut tree (now widely known as the 'conker'), is a favourite playground pastime among children and is traditionally played in September and October. Sadly, in recent years health and safety spoilsports have tried to ban the game on the grounds that a player might be injured (though serious injuries are so rare as to be immeasurable). There have even been attempts to have horse chestnut trees chopped down to prevent children obtaining conkers from them. Once the conker has been taken from its prickly casing, it is pieced with a skewer and a piece of string is threaded through the middle and then secured at one end. Each player has a conker hanging on a string and players take turns at hitting their opponent's conker. Once a crack has been made in a conker's casing, the end is usually swift. The conker which is to be hit must be held perfectly still, and quite firmly (so that when it is hit the string is not pulled out of the hand). If the strings tangle then the first player to shout 'strings' gets an extra shot. With numerous variations the game continues until one of the conkers is destroyed. The victorious conker then takes on the scores of all its previous victims. So, for example, if a new conker defeats one that has defeated six previous conkers then the victor will have a score of seven (and be known as a 'seven-er'). It is possible, in this way, for competitors to acquire conkers with quite considerable scores. When selecting a conker to play with, children sometimes drop possibles into a bucket of water. The conkers which sink, being denser, are usually stronger and harder. Old conkers, sometimes several years old, are also often harder than brand new, shiny ones. Some competitors bake their conkers in the oven, or soak them in vinegar. It is claimed that it is possible to harden a conker in this way. The World Conker Championships are held each year at Ashton in Northamptonshire. Competitors are not allowed to use their own conkers but must use seeds which have been gathered and strung by the organisers. The first recorded game of conkers was played in 1848 on the Isle of Wight and was based on a 15th century game which was played with hazelnuts. Conkers is played only in England, or by Englishmen abroad.

3. Eton Wall Game
This curious game is played only at Eton College on November 30th. One team consists of 70 boys who are scholars and who receive their education at reduced fees. The other team consists of the remaining 1,100 boys whose parents pay full fees. The aim is to 'boss' or score a goal by getting the ball into the 'calx' or territory owned by the other side. One 'calx' is a chalk mark on a wall. The other 'calx' is a chalk mark on a tree. It is rare for a goal to be scored and many decades can go by without the scorers being troubled.

4. Bottle kicking
This annual contest, a type of football without much in the way of rules, takes place between the villages of Hallaton and Medbourne in Leicestershire. The match is always played on Easter Monday and dates back to the time when a piece of land was left to the rector on condition that he and his successors provided two hare pies, 'a sufficiency of ale' and two dozen penny loaves to be fought for. The proceedings begin with a church service. After this the pies are taken onto Hare Pie Bank where contestants 'scramble' for them. When the pies have been well and truly fought over, the contestants prepare for the bottle kicking. A small wooden cask filled with beer (known as a bottle) is dropped three times by the Bottle Keeper. After the third drop, two teams (each consisting of any number of players) try to kick or carry the bottle over their own boundary. The winners keep the beer. Once the first cask has been won there are two more to be fought for (though the second 'bottle' contains no beer). The

contents of the third 'bottle' are shared among the players of both teams. An 18th century rector tried to use the money for a worthier cause. He was quickly 'persuaded' to change his mind.

5. The Haxey Hood game

In the 13th century, Lady Mowbray, the wife of a rich landowner in Lincolnshire, lost her hood when riding to church. Twelve labourers found it and returned it to her. (It was presumably a very large and heavy hood). She was so touched by this honesty that she gave the village of Haxey a piece of land which is still called the Hoodland. She instructed that the rent from the land should be used to pay for the purchase of a hood and that the hood would be competed for by twelve villagers wearing scarlet jerkins and caps. The competition starts at 2 p.m. on Plough Monday on the Church Green. An elected villager called King Boggon carries 13 willow wands bound together with 13 bands of willow and wears a tall hat decorated with flowers. He is accompanied by 12 Boggons, wearing red jackets and hats and by a Fool who has a blackened face and wears a costume with paper streamers attached to his back. The Fool recounts the origin of the game and while he is talking the paper streamers are lit. A match is also put to some damp straw at the man's feet. This is called Smoking the Fool. When the fire has been extinguished the Boggons lead the way to the top of Haxey Hill. The King Boggon then throws up the first hood – which is in reality a tightly bound roll of sacking. The man who catches the hood tries to carry it to the nearest public house where he will be given a shilling. Naturally, the other Boggons try to catch him. If they succeed then the hood is returned to the King Boggon who throws it up into the air again. Twelve hoods are distributed in this way. The 13th hood, a proper one made of leather, is then thrown up into the air and something called the Sway begins. The Sway is open to far more people and rival teams, each of which may contain hundreds of people, try to carry the hood into one of three local inns. Once the hood is taken into a pub there are free drinks all round and the hood remains in the winning pub until the next Haxey Day.

6. Cheese Rolling for Boys

A downhill race run annually in the Cotswolds on Whit Monday.

A specially made cheese is rolled down the one-in-three gradient of Cooper's Hill, near Birdlip in Gloucestershire. When the starter (dressed in a white beaver hat and an ancient smock) gives the word the competitors (all boys) run down the hill to catch the cheese. The winner keeps it.

GARDENS

The English are renowned for their gardens and for their love of them. There is no other nationality in the world that 'does' gardens as beautifully as the English 'do' theirs. Here are England's dozen most magnificent gardens:

1. Kew Gardens
The Royal Botanic Gardens at Kew, seven miles to the southwest of central London, are largely the creation of British explorer and naturalist, Joseph Banks. However, it was Augusta, Princess of Wales, who helped make the project possible by laying out a portion of her estate as a botanic garden in 1759. The gardens were donated to the nation in 1840.

2. Sissinghurst Castle Garden, Kent
The beautiful gardens at Sissinghurst were the creation of Vita Sackville-West and her husband, Sir Harold Nicholson. The gardens were first opened to the public in 1938.

3. Stowe Landscape Garden, Buckinghamshire
Stowe contains more than 40 monuments and temples, and is said to be one of the greatest landscaped gardens in England.

4. Hidcote Manor Garden, Gloucestershire
A beautiful Arts and Crafts garden, and the creation of self-taught gardener, Lawrence Johnston, who spent 41 years creating one of England's most beautiful gardens.

5. RHS Garden Wisley, Surrey

Wisley was given to the Royal Horticultural Society in 1903 by Sir Thomas Hanbury. There is a magnificent glasshouse at Wisley that is the size of 10 tennis courts and is 40ft high. The Glasshouse contains an amazing collection of plants.

6. Biddulph Grange Garden, Staffordshire

Fifteen acres of beautiful themed gardens which were designed by horticulturalist, James Bateman.

7. Studley Royal Water Garden, Yorkshire

This spectacular Georgian water garden, which contains an exquisite neo-classical building called the Temple of Piety, was the creation of the Aislabie family.

8. Oxford Botanic Garden, Oxfordshire

Founded in 1621, it is the oldest botanic garden in England, and contains around 7,000 different types of plant.

9. Leonardslee Gardens, Sussex

Famous for the azaleas and rhododendrons, these gardens were first begun by Sir Edmund Loder in the late 19th century.

10. Trelissick Garden, Cornwall

Largely created by the Copeland family in the 1930s. The garden is renowned for its collection of tender and exotic plants.

11. Westbury Court Garden, Gloucestershire

This beautiful Dutch water garden is believed to be home to England's oldest evergreen oak.

12. Mottisfont Abbey Gardens, Hampshire

The internationally renowned walled gardens at Mottisfont are home to the National Collection of Old-fashioned Roses.

GIFTS

The following are gifts that England gave to the world:

1. The English language
2. Imperial measures
3. The principle of fair play
4. The Magna Carta
5. The Law
6. A sense of decency and honour
7. Cricket (and all other sports)
8. Democracy
9. A free press
10. Parliament
11. Stamps, trains, aeroplanes, cars and just about everything else
12. Spotted Dick pudding

HAWTHORN, MIKE

World motor racing champion Mike Hawthorn used to wear a bow tie when driving in Grand Prix events. There were few greater sights in sport than that of Hawthorn racing his Ferrari at 160mph with his bow tie flapping in the wind.

HENRY VIII'S WIVES

King Henry VIII's first wife was Catherine of Aragon. She was a Roman Catholic who had been married to King Henry's elder brother, Prince Arthur. The prince died shortly after they were married, and Catherine went on to marry her brother-in-law, King Henry VIII, in 1509.

Unfortunately, over the years, Catherine of Aragon proved to be a disappointment to King Henry as she failed to produce a much desired and needed male heir. Catherine's first child was a boy but sadly he did not survive infancy.

The continuing disappointment of Catherine's inability to produce a son, combined with the fact that the King had become totally infatuated with Anne Boleyn (one of Catherine of Aragon's maids of honour) caused King Henry to question the legitimacy of his marriage to her. Henry and his advisers pointed out that according to the biblical book of Leviticus, any man who marries his brother's widow will be punished by being childless (even though Catherine of Aragon had a daughter).

Catherine of Aragon argued with great sincerity that her very short marriage to Henry's brother, Arthur, was never consummated and, therefore, no sin had been committed.

King Henry VIII appealed to Rome time and time again for his marriage to Catherine to be annulled on the grounds that it was illegal to marry a brother's widow (even though they had been given papal dispensation to marry) but Pope Clement VII refused to allow an annulment to allow Henry to get rid of his Catholic wife. The continued refusal by the Pope to allow Henry to get rid of Catherine motivated the split between the English church and Rome.

Eventually, Henry VIII unilaterally declared his marriage to Catherine of Aragon dissolved, persuading Thomas Cranmer, the newly appointed Archbishop of Canterbury, to decree that the marriage was null and void. (Thomas More had resigned, refusing to countenance divorce or annulment and he went on to be executed by Henry and to then become a saint.) In 1534, an Act of Supremacy was passed by Parliament recognising King Henry VIII as the Supreme Head of the Church of England.

Henry married the pregnant Anne Boleyn in a secret wedding ceremony in 1533. Anne Boleyn was never a popular Queen. She was looked upon by the people as the 'Great Whore' who had stolen King Henry VIII away from his long-standing first wife, the Spanish Catherine of Aragon.

Anne didn't last long, although she gave Henry a daughter who was called Elizabeth.

Wanting a reason that would free him of his wife because he had grown to despise her, and believed that his marriage to her was cursed because she had failed to produce a male heir, King Henry VIII had Protestant Queen Anne Boleyn beheaded at the Tower of London on 19th May 1536, for alleged multiple adultery and for incest with her own brother.

King Henry's determination to dispose of his wife was strengthened even further when he fell in love with Jane Seymour who was one of Anne Boleyn's maids of honours. (The young Elizabeth, who was to become Elizabeth I was not yet three years of age when her mother was executed.)

Henry VIII was said to have been devastated and heartbroken when Jane Seymour died shortly after giving birth to the son who would become Edward VI. Henry even made arrangements to be buried next to his beloved Jane after his death. The death of Jane Seymour did not, however, prevent him from marrying three more times.

Less than three years after Jane Seymour's death, King Henry VIII married Anne of Cleves, whom Thomas Cromwell, the King's Chief Minister and an ancestor of Oliver Cromwell, helped find for him. King Henry, who had only ever seen a portrait of his new queen, was dissatisfied with her appearance in the flesh and, therefore, had his marriage annulled. The King, who was by now fat and paranoid, was reported to have described Anne of Cleves as a 'Flanders Mare' which was probably a bit of a cheek considering that his waist measurement was now 54 inches. Thomas Cromwell was executed shortly afterwards, which just goes to show how dangerous pimping can be.

King Henry then went on to marry Anne Boleyn's cousin, Catherine Howard, in 1540. In less than two years of marriage, he had her executed on the grounds of adultery and married his sixth and final wife, Catherine Parr, in 1543. She had been married twice before. To everyone's surprise this Queen lasted longer than the King. He died in 1547, at the age of 55. Catherine Parr lasted until 1548 when she died shortly after giving birth to her next husband's daughter.

HOT TODDY

The English invented the Hot Toddy. (Not surprising, considering the weather.) The Hot Toddy is an excellent and warming drink for cold winter evenings. For best enjoyment the Hot Toddy should be prepared and drunk after a long walk in cold weather.

The recipe which follows is a traditional English Recipe for Spiced Hot Toddy, which originated in the village of Bilbury in Devon. (Serving For One)

1. Pour three table spoonfuls of the best whisky you can find into a Russian tea glass.

2. Add one teaspoonful of honey

3. Add a squeeze of lemon juice

4. Add three cloves

5. Add a teaspoonful of cinnamon

6. Add half a slice of fresh orange

7. Add a pinch of nutmeg

8. Pour in very hot water

9. Stir with a cinnamon stick

10. Inhale the vapour for a few moments

11. Find somewhere quiet, preferably close to a roaring log fire

12. Sip slowly and enjoy

HP SAUCE

HP Sauce, which has a malt vinegar base blended with fruits and spices was originally named Garton's Sauce after the creator of the sauce, a grocer living in Nottingham, called Frederick Gibson Garton. On learning that his sauce was being served in the canteen at the Houses of Parliament, F.G. Garton decided to call his sauce Garton's HP Sauce. And it was in 1896 that F.G. Garton registered that name for the sauce.

Garton handed over the recipe and brand to the owner of the

Midland Vinegar Company, Edwin Samson Moore who had been looking for a popular sauce to market. Edwin Moore bought the brand name and the recipe for £150. He also wrote off the debt Garton owed the Midland Vinegar Company.

During the 1960s and 1970s, HP Sauce was called 'Wilson's gravy' after Prime Minister Harold Wilson was rumoured to pour the sauce over his food.

ICONS

England has a long history and has more history than any other country on earth. Here are three dozen English icons:

1. Big Ben
2. Big breakfasts
3. Black cabs in London
4. Blackpool Tower
5. Bowler hats
6. Buckingham Palace
7. Cricket
8. Cups of tea
9. Deckchairs
10. Fish and chips
11. Irony
12. Jeeves and Wooster books by P.G. Wodehouse
13. Jerusalem (the poem)
14. London Eye
15. Lords Cricket Ground
16. Magna Carta
17. Morris Dancing
18. Oak trees
19. Public houses

20. Punch and Judy

21. Red post boxes

22. Red telephone boxes

23. River Thames

24. Roast Beef and Yorkshire Pudding

25. Robin Hood

26. Rolls Royce

27. Saint George

28. Sand castles on the beach

29. Stonehenge

30. *Three Men in a Boat* by Jerome K Jerome

31. Tower of London

32. Westminster Abbey

33. White Cliffs of Dover

34. Wimbledon Tennis Club

35. Windsor Castle

36. *Winnie the Pooh* by A. A. Milne

IMPERIAL MEASUREMENTS

Imperial measurements are the traditional way to measure things in England. This system of units was first defined in the Weights and Measures Act of 1824 and gradually brought into use throughout the Empire and the Colonies (including the United States of America). Some members of the modern bureaucracy have, without success, tried to outlaw traditional English measures.

Standard English Measures of Length:
    8 inches = 1 link
    12 inches = 1 foot
    3 feet = 1 yard
    25 links = 1 pole
    5 ½ yards = 1 pole

4 poles = 1 chain
10 chains = 1 furlong
8 furlongs = 1 mile (or 1760 yards)

(Some of these measurements, although official, are a trifle vague. For example, a link is, strictly speaking, actually just a tiny bit less than 8 inches in length.)

Other traditional English measures of length:
12 lines = 1 inch
3 inches = 1 palm
4 inches = 1 hand
18 inches = 1 cubit
2 feet 6 inches = 1 pace (military)
5 feet = 1 pace (geographic)
6 feet = 1 fathom
240 yards = 1 cable
3 miles = 1 league
1760 yards = 1 mile
2025 yards = 1 nautical mile
6075 yards = 1 league
60 nautical miles = 1 degree

Foreign measurements in yards:
Austrian mile = 8360 yards
Belgian post = 7981 yards
Danish mile = 8244 yards
Dutch mile = 6480 yards
French kilometre = 1093 yards
French myriametre = 10936 yards
French lieuve = 4263 yards
Irish mile = 2240 yards
Italian mile = 2236 yards
Portugese league = 6760 yards
Russian verst = 1167 yards
Scottish (old) mile = 1984 yards
Spanish league = 7410 yards
Swiss Stunde = 5773 yards
Vienna post mile = 8296 yards

English Measures for liquids, corn, etc.:
  5 ozs = 1 gill
  4 gills = 1 pint
  2 pints = 1 quart
  4 quarts = 1 gallon

English Measures for dry goods only:
  2 gallons = 1 peck
  4 pecks = 1 bushel
  8 bushels = 1 quarter
  10 quarters = 1 last

English Measures of surface:
  144 square inches = 1 square foot
  9 square feet = 1 square yard
  30¼ square yards = 1 square pole
  40 square poles = 1 rood
  4 roods = 1 acre
  640 acres = 1 square mile

There are some traditional and special measures of surface:
  36 square yards of stone, brick or slate work = 1 rood
  100 square feet of flooring = 1 square

There are some special divisions of avoirdupois weight used for measuring wool:
  2 stones = 1 tod
  6½ tods = 1 wey
  2 weys = 1 sack
  12 sacks = 1 last
  240 lbs = 1 pack

There are also special measures for hay and straw:
  36 lb straw = 1 truss
  60 lbs new hay (until Sept 1) = 1 truss
  56 lbs old hay (after Sept 1) = 1 truss
  36 trusses = 1 load

And for flour:
    14 pounds = 1 stone
    56 pounds = 1 bushel
    140 pounds = 1 boll
    112 pounds = 1 cwt
    2 and a half cwt = 1 sack

And wood:
    128 cubic feet of cut wood = 1 cord

Troy weights (used for measuring gold, silver, etc.):
    24 grains = 1 pennyweight
    20 pennyweights = 1 ounce
    12 ounces = 1 pound

N.B. As a tribute to our imperial measurements, lists in this book are in dozens or half dozens.

INVENTIONS AND DISCOVERIES

All the best things in life originated in England. All the next best things in life were improved in England. In the 19th century, England led the way in roads, railways and iron ships. The first trains ran in England and England had the first houses lit by electric light. The English invented just about everything worth inventing (far more than any other nationality.) Here is a list of just a few of the great English inventions and discoveries. The men and women below are the backbone of the industrial revolution, the spirit of the English Renaissance and the soul of England.

    Absolute zero temperature – Lord Kelvin
    Atomic theory – John Dalton
    Calculus – Isaac Newton
    Car – Richard Trevithick
    Carbonated water in 1767 – Joseph Priestley
    Cats' eyes road markings – Percy Shaw

Champagne – Christopher Merrett
Chemical electrolysis – Humphry Davy
Circulation of the blood – William Harvey
Computer – Charles Babbage
Computer programme – Ada Lovelace
Concrete – John Smeaton
Crossword puzzle – Arthur Wynne
Democratic government – Oliver Cromwell
Diamagnetism – Michael Faraday
Diving bell – Edmund Halley
Dynamo – Michael Faraday
Economic theory – William Petty
Electric lightbulb – Joseph Wilson Swan
Electric telegraph – Charles Wheatstone
Electricity – Michael Faraday
Electromagnet – William Sturgeon
Electrons – Joseph Thomson
Evolution – Charles Dawrin
Fire extinguisher – George Manby
Flushing toilet – John Harington
Friction match – John Walker
Glider – George Cayley
Hooke's law of elasticity – Robert Hooke
Hormones – William Bayliss and Ernest Starling
Hovercraft – Christopher Cockerell
Hydraulic press – Joseph Bramah
Hydrogen – Henry Cavendish
Jet engine – Frank Whittle
Jigsaw puzzle – John Spilsbury
Knitting machine – Rev William Lee
Law of conservation of energy – James Joule
Law of gravity – Isaac Newton
Lawnmower – Edwin Budding
Laws of Motion – Isaac Newton
Lead Crystal – George Ravenscroft
Magnifying glass – Roger Bacon
Manned flight – George Cayley
Maritime clock – John Harrison

Mass production – Richard Arkwright
Mass spectrometer – Francis Aston
Matches – John Walker
Mortality tables – Edmond Halley
Moving pictures – Eadweard Muybridge
Neutrons – James Chadwick
Orbiting comets – Edmund Halley
Pencil eraser – Joseph Priestley
Photography – William Henry Fox Talbot
Plastic – Alexander Parkes
Polythene – Reginald Gibson and Eric Fawcett
Portland cement – Joseph Aspdin
Postage stamp – Rowland Hill
Propeller – Francis Pettit Smith
Radar – Robert Alexander Watson-Watt
Railway locomotive – George Stephenson
Red blood cells – Robert Hooke
Rubber – Thomas Hancock
Sandwich – Earl of Sandwich
Satellites – Arthur C. Clarke
Seed drill – Jethro Tull
Sewing machine – Thomas Saint
Spectacles – Roger Bacon
Spinning jenny – James Hargreaves
Stainless steel – Harry Brearley
Steam Engine – Thomas Savery
Steam turbine – Charles Parsons
Submarine – William Bourne
Synthetic dyes – William Henry Perkin
Syringe – Christopher Wren
Traffic lights – J. P. Knight
Tuning fork – John Shore
Universal joint – Robert Hooke
Vaccination – Edward Jenner
Vacuum cleaner – H. E. Booth
World Wide Web – Tim Berners Lee

IRON DUKE

The Duke of Wellington was nicknamed the 'iron duke' not for his military victories (which included the defeat of Napoleon at Waterloo in 1815) but because he had iron shutters fitted onto his windows to prevent them from being smashed by rioters during the parliamentary reform crisis in the 19th century. The Duke of Wellington was a popular general but he was not a popular Prime Minister. He is immortalised by the boot which he made popular and which now bears his name (although the ones he wore were rather stouter and better looking than the rubbery items sold today).

JERUSALEM

Jerusalem has become an unofficial English anthem. The words were written by William Blake (1757-1827) and the music was composed by Hubert Parry (1848-1918). The two were first brought together in 1915.

And did those feet in ancient times,
Walk upon England's mountains green?
And was the holy Lamb of God,
On England's pleasant pastures seen?
And did the countenance divine,
Shine forth upon our clouded hills?
And was Jerusalem builded here,
Among these dark Satanic mills?

Bring me my bow of burning gold!
Bring me my arrows of desire!
Bring me my spear! O clouds unfold!
Bring me my chariot of fire!
I will not cease from mental fight,
Nor shall my sword sleep in my hand,
Till we have built Jerusalem,
In England's green and pleasant land.

LANCASHIRE HOT POT

Lancashire Hot Pot consists of lamb, onions, carrots and a top layer of sliced potatoes. It is thought that Lancashire Hot Pot has its origins in the Lancashire cotton industry. Because this simple dish cooks rather slowly, female mill workers would put the dish in their ovens before setting off to work and by the time they returned home, it would be ready to eat.

LANGUAGE (ENGLISH)

1. More countries around the world now speak English than any other language. Those countries owe their civilisations to England.
2. There are over 500,000 words in the English language, compared to German which has only 185,000 and French which has less than 100,000.
3. One billion people now speak English as their first language.
4. Over four fifths of the Internet and e-mail are in English.
5. Over 200 million Chinese are learning English.
6. India now has more native English speakers than England.
7. When the spacecraft Voyager 1 went deep into the solar system it carried a message from the United Nations on behalf of 147 countries. The message was in English.
8. English contains bits and pieces from over a hundred other languages.
9. The longest word not to repeat a letter is 'uncopyrightable'
10. The letters '-ough' can be pronounced nine different ways. The following sentence contains them all: 'A thoughtful, dough-faced, rough-coated ploughman wandered through the streets of Scarborough; after falling into a slough, he coughed and hiccoughed for hours.'
11. The word 'bookkeeper' is the only English word to contain three consecutive double letters.
12. No other language has as many ways of saying the same thing.

LAWS

Peculiar Laws of Old England

Some of the laws of old England have never officially been repealed, though many have been superseded and are now non-operational.

1. If anyone dies in the Houses of Parliament, their body must be removed before a death certificate can be issued otherwise he or she is entitled to a state funeral. This is because the Palace of Westminster is a royal palace.

2. It is against the law for a member of parliament to enter the House of Commons wearing a full suit of armour.

3. In Hertford, there is an old law which allows a woman to throw away her husband's collection of pornography if she wishes.

4. By law, London cab drivers have to ask every passenger whether they have small pox or the plague. It is illegal for a black cab in the city of London to carry corpses or rabid dogs.

5. George I passed an Act which states that 'severest penaltys will be suffered by any commoner who doth permit his animal to have carnal knowledge of a pet of the Royal House'.

6. It used to be the law that all males over the age of 14 years in England had to do two hours of longbow practice – supervised by the local clergy – every weekend.

7. Under the '1891 Slander of Women Act' it is illegal to 'impute unchastity or adultery' to women living in England, Ireland and Wales.

8. In Bristol, there is a by-law which bans couples from having sex underneath a car. There is another bizarre law in Bristol which ruled that couples are not allowed to kick a dog out of bed during lovemaking. A dog is apparently legally entitled to be a voyeur.

9. In Liverpool, there is an old law which forbids children to look up the dresses of mannequins in shop windows.

10. It was, for many years, legal for an Englishman to shoot a Welshman on a Sunday in the quadrangle of Hereford Cathedral – as long as he used a bow and arrow. Similarly, there used to

be an old law which made it legal to shoot a Scotsman with a bow and arrow in the city of York (though this was only legal if done after dark, and within the city walls).

11. It used to be illegal in Newmarket to blow your nose in the street.

12. In Somerset, there used to be a by-law which prohibited people from wearing the same clothes on a Sunday that they had worn during the week.

LE MANS VICTORY

Two heroic Englishmen, Sammy Davis and Dr J. D. Benjafield were driving their Bentley at Le Mans in June 1927 when the car (known as 'Old No 7') was involved in a massive crash. The Bentley was severely damaged. The front of the car, axle, cross-member, mudguard and one front wheel were all distorted. Only one headlamp worked. The battery had to be tied onto the running board and the brakes weren't working properly. The steering was 'odd' and had no return action. Eighteen hours later, the two men having driven through darkness and pouring rain, the Bentley crossed the finishing line with Sammy Davis at the wheel, a mudguard flapping like a broken wing. The car had covered 1,472 miles at an average of over 61mph.

The second place car was more than 200 miles behind them.

LITTLE ENGLANDERS

Those who use the term 'Little Englander' as a term of abuse for people who love England are woefully ignorant. The term dates from the Boer War and refers to people who were, at the time, opposed to the British Empire and who were anti-imperialist in their attitude. 'Little Englanders' wanted the English to stop taking over the world. The Little Englanders believed that no nation was superior enough to rule another nation. At the time such folk were regarded as unpatriotic.

LLOYD GEORGE, DAVID (1863-1945)

David Lloyd George was Prime Minister from 1916-1922. He is arguably the most famous Welshman who ever lived.

It is not widely known but he was actually born in Manchester.

LONDON EYE
Half a Dozen Facts

1. The London Eye is located at the western end of Jubilee Gardens on the South Bank of the River Thames in London. The Eye (as it is sometimes known) gives spectacular views of up to 25 miles. The London Eye has been designed to give passengers 360-degree panoramic views.

2. The London Eye (also known as the Millennium Wheel) opened to the public in March 2000. Over 3.5 million people visit the London Eye each year.

3. The London Eye was the idea of two architects, David Marks and Julia Barfield.

4. The London Eye has 32 completely enclosed capsules. The 32 capsules represent the 32 London boroughs. Each glass pod can hold as many as 28 people.

5. Each capsule contains emergency supplies of water, blankets and even commodes.

6. It takes approximately 30 minutes for the Eye to perform a full circle. The Eye moves so slowly that customers just hop on and off as it comes round.

THE MAGNA CARTA – HISTORY

The words Magna Carta are Latin for 'Great Charter'.

England's Magna Carta is the most important document in the English language. It is England's version of a constitution; a legal document, signed in 1215, which promised the people of England liberty and freedom from tyranny.

The man who signed the document, King John, was England's most unpopular King. He was a despot whose corrupt administration and crushingly high taxes alienated and united all groups of people. (King John was an exceedingly unpleasant man. Once, in a fit of pique, he tried to convert England to Islam.)

The man behind the Magna Carta was Stephen Langton, the Archbishop of Canterbury at the time. It was he who united the nation and encouraged King John's barons to demand that the King sign a document guaranteeing rights for Englishmen.

The barons, who were furious that the King had introduced high taxes and was abusing his feudal rights, wanted to protect their privileges and limit the King's power by law. However, the Magna Carta wasn't just concerned with the barons' rights; the document contained clauses that, today, are the foundation of democracy. The Magna Carta was created to curb the power of King John and to give rights to English citizens.

Here are a dozen things you should know about the Magna Carta:

1. The scribes who wrote the Magna Carta used a gall based ink created by tapping into the galls which grow on the bark of oak trees. These develop when a wasp stings the tree to lay its egg. The tree stops the poison spreading by forming a small nut around it. That's the gall. If you tap the gall you obtain a clear acidic fluid which, when used as ink on vellum or parchment, etches itself into the material. If you add soot or iron salts to the ink it turns dark brown – almost black if mixed well.

2. The pens used were quills, taken from the flight feathers of swans or geese. Every ten lines or so, the writer would trim his quill with a penknife (that's where the name comes from) and dip it into the ink.

3. When originally prepared, the Magna Carta was called the Charter of Liberties. It was renamed a few years later to distinguish it from the shorter legislative document the Forest Charter.

4. No one knows how many copies of the Magna Carta were made, but only four remain. One is in Salisbury Cathedral, one in Lincoln Cathedral and two are in the British Library. One of these lies under bullet-proof glass and can be viewed by members of the public.

5. The Magna Carta contains 63 clauses.

6. The authors of the American Declaration of Independence read the Magna Carta before creating their document.

7. The Magna Carta was the basis of British democracy and justice for 800 years.

8. The Magna Carta is regarded throughout the world as the most important foundation stone of modern freedom and democracy. Many countries have based their constitutions upon the Magna Carta.

9. The Magna Carta is not illustrated or illuminated. It is almost but not quite square. When originally created it had a green and black wax seal attached to the bottom.

10. The Magna Carta, which was written in Latin, was reissued three times during Henry III's (King John's son) reign. And it was the 1225 version that became law.

11. On 12 October 1297, Henry III's son and heir, Edward I, reissued the Magna Carta as part of a statute reconfirming his father's shortened version of the 1225 document. The Magna Carta was then formally recognised as the law of the land.

12. In recent years, the Magna Carta has become largely redundant and irrelevant because of treaties signed with the European Union. The basic long-established rights fought for by Stephen Langton and the barons were abolished by governments which have handed authority over Englishmen and Englishwomen to European bureaucrats. This has been done without the approval of the English people.

The most important clauses in the Magna Carta include these:

1. 'No free man shall be taken or imprisoned or deprived or outlawed or exiled or in any way ruined, nor will we go or send against him, except by the lawful judgement of his peers or by the law of the land.'

2. 'The city of London shall enjoy all its ancient liberties and free customs, both by land and by water. We also will and grant that all other cities, boroughs, towns, and ports shall enjoy all their liberties and free customs.'

3. 'For a trivial offence, a free man shall be fined only in proportion to the degree of his offence, and for a serious offence correspondingly, but not so heavily as to deprive him of his livelihood. In the same way, a merchant shall be spared his merchandise, and a husbandman the implements of his husbandry, if they fall upon the mercy of a royal court. None of these fines shall be imposed except by the assessment on oath of reputable men of the neighbourhood.'

4. 'No sheriff, royal official, or other person shall take horses or carts for transport from any free man, without his consent.'

5. 'No free man shall be seized or imprisoned, or stripped of his rights or possessions, or outlawed or exiled, or deprived of his standing in any other way, nor will we proceed with force against him, or send others to do so, except by the lawful judgement of his equals or by the law of the land.'

6. 'To no man will we sell, or deny, or delay, right or justice.'

MANNED FLIGHT

In 1853, English baronet George Cayley constructed the world's first full-size flying machine, a glider, which was flown across Brompton Dale. It had a wing area of 300 square feet and was the world's first heavier-than-air machine to fly. There is some confusion about the identity of the pilot, though it is generally believed that the first aviator was either Cayley's coachman, footman or butler. Alternatively, it may have been his grandson who made the flight. The flight, the first ever made, was described in the *Encyclopaedia Britannica* of 1855.

George Cayley (1773-1857) was born and died in Yorkshire. He was the founder of the science of aerodynamics, the pioneer of aerial navigation and the designer of the first modern aeroplane. He was the first person to understand the principles of flight and worked over half a century before people now often credited with inventing the aeroplane. (The Wright Brothers, often described by American writers as the first men to fly, did not get into the air with a heavier-than-air machine until 1903 – nearly half a century after Cayley's death).

Cayley started developing his ideas about the theory of flight, and his plans for an aeroplane, when he was still at school. In 1799, he invented the concept of the modern aeroplane as a fixed wing flying machine with separate systems for propulsion, lift and control. Five years later he built his first model glider, which had a pair of large monoplane wings near the front and a small tailplane at the rear. The tailplane consisted of a vertical fin and horizontal stabilisers. In 1809, he published groundbreaking aerodynamic research in his treatise *On Aerial Navigation* which was published in the *Journal of Natural Philosophy, Chemistry and the Arts*. He studied wing design, invented cambered wings and invented streamlining and stability in the air. He also investigated the aerodynamic forces of drag, lift and thrust. Sometime in the 1840's he designed and built a triplane powered with flappers. An unknown ten-year-old boy, chosen for his light weight, flew this aeroplane.

MAP OF LONDON

Phyllis Pearsall (1906-1996) designed and created the first A to Z map of London single-handed. She walked 3,000 miles to do it. She produced 10,000 copies which didn't sell to begin with. Eventually, W.H. Smith took 250 copies which she delivered in a wheelbarrow herself. (She presumably knew the quickest route to get there.)

MARMALADE

In 1874, a woman called Sarah Jane Cooper used to sell her surplus hand-made marmalade (the recipe of which was believed to have been handed down to her by her mother) in the shop that she and her husband Frank ran in 83-84 High Street, Oxford. The marmalade was such a hit with the public, especially with students that queues used to form regularly outside the shop. Eventually, the demand for the marmalade was so huge that Frank Cooper decided to open a factory in Park End Street, Oxford.

When the famous explorer Robert Scott went to Antarctica, he took some of Frank Cooper's Oxford marmalade with him. Years later, the marmalade was found and was said to still be in good condition.

MONARCH (HOW TO TALK TO AN ENGLISH MONARCH)

1. When meeting the Monarch (whether King or Queen) a woman should curtsy. A man should bow, although these days it is acceptable to bow the head only.

2. The correct formal address to either a King or Queen is, in the first instance, 'Your Majesty'. If the conversation continues for longer than this, a King should be addressed as 'Sir' and a Queen should be addressed as 'Ma'am' (pronounced to rhyme with jam).

3. You should never refer to the Monarch as 'you'. For example, you should not say 'I hope you are having a nice day' but instead 'I hope Your Majesty is having a nice day'.

MORRIS DANCING (THE QUINTESSENTIAL ENGLISH DANCE)

A Dozen Facts

1. The original purpose of Morris dancing was as a ritual to demonstrate a man's virility.

2. In the early 21st century, there were 800 troupes or sides of dancers in England – nearly all male.

3. Morris dancing is believed to be a remnant of Druidic fertility rituals. The bells, clashing sticks and fluttering handkerchiefs serve to frighten away malevolent spirits.

4. The earliest recorded Morris dancing in England took place in London on 19th May 1448 when 'Moryssh daunsers' were paid 7 shillings for their services.

5. Shakespeare wrote Morris dancing into *All's Well That Ends Well*.

6. Traditionally, Morris dancing was performed on May Day.

7. King James I's *Book of Sports* included 'Morris dances and the setting up of May-poles' as acceptable activities which could be enjoyed on Sundays.

8. Oliver Cromwell regarded Morris dancing as 'potentially seditious'. In an Ordinance dated 1654, the staging of Morris dancing, and other 'licentious practices', was regarded as sufficient grounds to 'eject Scandalous, Ignorant and Insufficient Ministers and Schoolmasters' from their jobs.

9. Morris dancing revived under Charles II but withered somewhat by the end of the 19th century, though Morris dancers did perform for Queen Victoria's Golden Jubilee celebrations in 1887.

10. Costumes vary around the country. In the Cotswolds, dancers dress in hats decorated with flowers, bells below their knees, black shoes and white shirts and trousers with a tunic. In the northwest, dancers wear clogs. In the West of England, close to Wales, dancers wear black top hats decorated with pheasant feathers, and blacken their faces.

11. The leader of a side of Morris dancers is called the Squire. The teacher, who trains the dancers, is called the Foreman. The bookings secretary or treasurer will be known as the Bagman. Many dance sides have a fool, a beast or a hobby – a dancer who performs alone but alongside the group.

12. Morris dancing is extremely complicated. Ballet dancers are sometimes encouraged to practise Morris dancing because it helps them develop quick, nimble feet.

MUSTARD

Colman's Original English Mustard

In 1814, a Norfolk flour miller called Jeremiah Colman advertised the mustard which he made at his mill in Stoke Holy Cross just south of Norwich. He made what has become England's best known mustard from a blend of white and brown mustard seeds.

In 1823, Mr Colman took his adopted nephew James into partnership with him and the firm was named J & J Colman.

The firm improved working life for their employees by opening a school for their children to attend. The firm also employed the nation's first industrial nurse.

A popular rival mustard manufacturer, Keen Robinson & Company (hence the well-known saying 'as keen as mustard' – originally an advertising slogan), was bought by the Colman firm in 1903.

The brand's trademark, the bull's head that is depicted on the Colman's mustard label, was introduced in 1855.

MYTTON, JOHN (1796-1834)

John Mytton was the most eccentric Englishman of all time. He was born in 1796 and died just 38 years later in 1834. But he crammed a good deal into his short life. He was described by his family as 'high spirited'. Here are two dozen examples of his high spirited nature:

1. He was asked to leave Westminster School after a year for 'fighting with the masters'. He then went to Harrow where he lasted three days.

2. When it was decided that he should attend Cambridge University he arranged for 2,000 bottles of port to be ready for his arrival. In the end he changed his mind and didn't go to Cambridge. There is no record of what happened to the port.

3. On his 21st birthday, Mytton inherited £60,000 and estates worth £18,000. This was a vast sum at the time. However, in the remaining 17 years of his life he got through more than £500,000 and ended up bankrupt.

4. He spent a year in the 7th Hussars. Most of the time he was gambling, drinking and racing. At a farewell dinner he persuaded his horse, Baronet, to leap the fully laden mess table.

5. In 1819, Mytton decided to seek election as MP for Shrewsbury. While campaigning he walked round the constituency with £10 notes pinned to his hat. As the notes were taken so they were replaced. Mytton spent £10,000 in this way and won the election by 384 votes to 287.

6. When Mytton got to the House of Commons he found the first debate he attended uninteresting. He left and never went back.

7. Every morning Mytton drank five bottles of port before lunch. If the port ran out (not something that happened often) he would drink eau-de-Cologne or lavender water.

8. Mytton liked to drive his gig into rabbit holes at high speed to see if it would turn over. (It invariably did.) When a passenger complained that his carriage driving was reckless and might overturn the carriage, Mytton scoffed and said: 'What? Never been upset in a gig? What a damned slow fellow you must have been all your life.' He then deliberately ran the carriage up a steep incline and overturned it so that the passenger could experience an 'upset'.

9. Mytton kept 60 cats which he dressed in liveries suitable to their breeds. He was even fonder of dogs and had 2,000 of those. When his favourite dog Tizer was losing a fight with a

friend's dog, Mytton bit the other dog's nose and held on until the dog gave in.

10. On one occasion, Mytton rode into his dining room in full hunting costume. To the alarm of his guests he was riding his pet brown bear called Nell at the time. When Mytton dug his spurs in, the bear bit him on the leg.

11. Mytton frequently took his favourite horse into the house, sat it by the fire and served it mulled port. Sadly, the horse did not have Mytton's capacity for alcohol. It died.

12. Mytton once replaced the last few pages of the local vicar's sermon with pages from the *Sporting Magazine*.

13. He once got his horse dealer drunk and put him to bed with two bull terriers and Nell, the brown bear. Mytton sent the same horse dealer to a banker in Shrewsbury, ostensibly to collect money for him. He gave the dealer a note to hand to the banker, who was also a governor of the local mental hospital. The note read: 'Sir, please admit the bearer, George Underhill, to the lunatic asylum. Your obedient servant, John Mytton.

14. When a tough Welsh miner tried to head off his hounds, Mytton leapt off his horse and challenged the man to a fistfight. After twenty rounds the miner gave in. Mytton congratulated the man and gave him half a sovereign.

15. When his creditors became a little too aggressive, Mytton moved to France. In a hotel in Calais he developed hiccups and decided to get rid of the problem by giving himself a fright. He set fire to his nightshirt. This cured the hiccups ('The hiccup is gone, by God!' he is reputed to have said.) but he was badly burned. Advised to stay in bed for a month he arranged to go out for dinner. But when his dining companion sent a two horse equipage for him, Mytton, covered in bandages, refused to get into it, claiming that he would sooner walk than ride in a carriage with less than four horses. Supported by two servants, he walked a mile and a half to dinner.

16. After being released from a debtor's prison in 1832, Mytton met an attractive young woman on Westminster Bridge. He asked her where she was going. She said she didn't know. Mytton offered

her £500 a year to live with him. She accepted and spent the last two years of his life with him in Calais.

17. On separate occasions, Mytton fought both dogs and bears armed with nothing more than his teeth.

18. In winter he went duck hunting in his nightshirt or, on occasion, completely naked.

19. He invented a game which involved chasing rats across a frozen pond while wearing skates.

20. He bet a friend that he could give him a 15-minute start and still beat him home on horseback. Mytton won easily by taking a short cut through a lake which he forced his horse to swim. If he had been thrown from his horse he would have drowned because he could not swim.

21. When out riding in bad weather, Mytton would knock on a cottage door and ask if his horse could dry off by the fire. Since he owned most of the local cottages he was never refused.

22. His wardrobe contained 700 pairs of boots, 150 pairs of riding breeches, 1,000 hats and nearly 3,000 shirts.

23. He died, in prison, from alcohol poisoning. He was just 38-years-old. More than 3,000 friends and acquaintances attended his funeral.

24. For some undisclosed reason, John Mytton was known to his friends as 'Mad Jack'.

NELSON, HORATIO (1758-1805)
A Dozen Facts

1. Born in Burnham Thorpe in Norfolk, Nelson entered the navy at the age of 12 and served in the West Indies from 1777 to 1783.

2. Nelson is remembered as the most successful fighting seaman of all time; the most skilled and audacious admiral in naval history.

3. Nelson achieved decisive victories, despite facing larger Franco-Spanish forces, through devising a dramatically new strategy.

4. The usual form of naval attack during the late 18th and early 19th centuries had always been to place the 'ships of the line' parallel to those of the enemy in what was known as 'line ahead'. Both sides would then fire broadsides at one another. Speed of firing and accuracy would eventually result in a sort of victory for one side. But relatively few ships were sunk by this method of fighting and the side which was losing could usually still sail away.

5. Nelson's tactical genius was first apparent in 1797 at the battle of St Vincent where he disobeyed orders (risking a court martial) and sailed out of line in order to intercept French vessels. His tactic was successful and instead of being court martialled he was knighted and promoted to Rear Admiral.

6. In 1798, at the Battle of the Nile, Nelson attacked from both sides, cut through the line of enemy ships and, in a pincer movement, captured 11 out of the enemy's 13 ships. It was a stunning victory.

7. In 1801, at Copenhagen, Nelson famously put his telescope to his weak eye and ignored a hesitant commanding officer to take a naval advantage from a prospective defeat.

8. It is a myth that Nelson was blind in one eye and another myth that he wore an eye patch. His eye looked 'normal' and worked reasonably well, though it had been damaged during fighting in Corsica in 1794. He did, however, have an eye-shade made into his hat to protect his good eye from the sun's rays.

9. At Trafalgar, on October 21st, 1805, Nelson used his knowledge and experience to create a meticulously designed battleplan. He told his captains to attack in two columns, at right angles to the Franco-Spanish enemy line. He foresaw that when he cut through the enemy lines his ships would be able to deliver devastating broadsides up and down a defenceless enemy line that was unable to return fire. The plan required great courage as well as vision. During their approach, the English ships were on the receiving end of continuous enemy broadsides from a much larger fleet. They could not return fire because they were sailing towards the enemy. Nelson's ships approached the enemy under full sail in order to minimise the time they would be under fire without being able to retaliate. The wind was lighter than

expected and it took 20 minutes for the English fleet to reach the enemy. Nelson's own ship, Victory, was severely damaged. But as the English ships cut through the Franco-Spanish lines, they discharged double loaded broadsides at the enemy. Heavy cannon fire, delivered at very short range, demolished the enemy ships and killed many of their crews. No English ships were lost but 18 ships from the French and Spanish fleets were captured.

10. During the battle of Trafalgar, as an inspiration to his men, Nelson walked around on deck wearing all his medals. He was an obvious target for sharp-shooters (snipers) in the rigging of the enemy ships. Shortly after the English ships had broken through the enemy line, and turned the battle in England's favour, a musket bullet from a sniper in the rigging of the French ship Redoutable hit Nelson and killed him.

11. Nelson's body was taken back to England, preserved in a cask of brandy and under armed guard.

12. Following a state funeral he was interred in the crypt of St Paul's Cathedral. He was buried in a coffin made with planks taken from the French ship L'Orient, which had been destroyed at the Battle of the Nile in 1798.

NEWTON, ISAAC (1642-1727)

A dozen and a half facts about the greatest scientist who ever lived:

1. Isaac Newton, the mathematician and physicist was born prematurely at Woolsthorpe Manor-house, Lincolnshire on Christmas Day in 1642. Isaac's father, whom Isaac was named after, never got to see his son for the uneducated but prosperous farmer had died three months before his child was born.

2. In 1659, Isaac's mother decided to take her son out of his school in Grantham so that he could manage the farm. Isaac proved utterly useless at this because the work didn't interest him. Instead of working on the farm, he was often found with his head stuck in a book. He could be absent-minded, in that way

academics are often said to be. One day he was in such deep thought whilst coming home from town that he didn't realise his horse had slipped out of its bridle. He walked all the way home totally oblivious to the fact that he was holding an empty bridle. Thankfully, with the help of the school principal, Mr Stokes, and Isaac's uncle, the Reverend William Ayscough, Isaac was sent back to his school in Grantham to continue his studies.

3. In 1661, (older than most of his fellow students because of his interrupted education), Isaac attended Trinity College Cambridge as a subsizar (carrying out menial tasks for wealthy students in order to earn his keep). Isaac largely ignored the official university syllabus and pursued his own studies. He immersed himself in the learning of René Descartes' Geometry (which inspired his love of the subject), the works of Aristotle, Thomas Hobbes, Franciscus van Schooten, John Wallis, Henry More, Robert Boyle and many other great intellects. Newton could absorb literature like a sponge and possessed amazing powers of concentration.

4. Newton worked hard at university, often staying up all night to study. Sadly, in 1665, a plague epidemic forced the university to close and Newton returned to Woolsthorpe. The 16 months away from university proved to be a very productive time for Newton. He discovered that white light is composed of many colours; he laid the foundations of the calculus; and considered the laws of universal gravity. Legend has it that it was seeing an apple fall in the orchard that triggered Newton into studying gravity. Whatever the truth is about the original idea, the theory of gravity took nearly 20 years of rumination. Newton collated his ideas about gravity two decades later in *Philosophiae Naturalis Principia Mathematica* (commonly known as *Principia*) – now regarded as the greatest book in the history of science.

5. Isaac Newton put himself forward as a candidate for a fellowship when the university reopened in 1667. He was elected a Minor Fellow of Trinity and was elected a Major Fellow after being awarded his Master's Degree in 1668. He concentrated most of his mental energy on optics. And in 1668, he constructed (with his own hands) the first functioning reflecting telescope, which later gave him great recognition in the scientific community.

6. In 1669, Newton was elected Lucasian Professor of Mathematics at Cambridge. He remained at the university, lecturing in most years, until 1696.

7. It was Newton's friend, Edmond Halley, who encouraged Newton to publish the book on gravity; he even financed its publication. As well as universal gravitation, *Principia* (published in 1687) contained Newton's three laws of motion and many other important ideas. It was this book that made Newton famous throughout Europe as the greatest scientific thinker of that time.

8. Through a series of experiments using glass prisms and a ray of sunlight, Newton proved that white light was made up of the colours of the rainbow and was not pure – a theory which people had believed for centuries.

9. Newton found the mechanics of vision and the nature of light fascinating. So great was his fascination that in order to investigate his theory of colours, he once carried out a hazardous experiment on himself which involved inserting a bodkin into his eye.

10. It wasn't until 1672 that Newton sent his first paper to the Royal Society containing details of his important experiment proving that white light is a mixture of many colours.

11. Newton's formula of calculus, devised during his productive 16 months away from university, was undoubtedly the single most important contribution to mathematics and one of the major scientific breakthroughs. Calculus made possible most of the subsequent progress in modern science and is used in everything from construction to electrical engineering. Through its two primary tools, the integral and the derivative, calculus allows scientists to calculate precisely rates of change and amounts of change in a system. Despite its importance, Newton's work on calculus went unpublished for over 30 years. Newton was often reluctant to have his work published for fear of criticism; which meant that a lot of his theories weren't made public until many years after he'd first thought of them.

12. Newton was elected Member of Parliament for the University of Cambridge in 1689. During his parliamentary career, Isaac Newton made just one speech, when he said: 'There's a bit of a draught. Can you close that window?'

13. In 1696, Newton was appointed Warden of the Mint, and in 1699 he was made Master of the Mint – an office he retained right up until his death. During his time at the Mint – a job which he put his heart and soul into – he did much to improve the organisation's efficiency and he went to great lengths to combat forgery (sending quite a number of counterfeiters to the gallows). Newton also supervised recoinage. Isaac Newton moved to Jermyn Street in London when he worked for the Mint.

14. In London, he invited his niece, Catherine Barton to run his household. Catherine Barton was charming, intelligent, beautiful and a brilliant conversationalist. Newton was very fond of her, and she caused quite a stir amongst London society.

15. In 1703, Newton was elected President of the Royal Society of London and was re-elected annually for the rest of his life.

16. In 1705, Isaac Newton was knighted by Queen Anne. He was the first scientist ever to be knighted.

17. Isaac Newton was an extraordinary man. He suffered two nervous breakdowns, was a keen student of alchemy (something he kept secret) and spent 25 years searching for the Philosopher's Stone. He studied Christianity extensively – he possessed 30 bibles in many languages – almost blinded himself by staring at the sun for hours during one of his experiments (for several days afterwards he had to stay in a darkened room until his eyesight returned to normal) and designed Queen Anne's Coronation Medal.

18. On March 20th 1727, Isaac Newton died at Kensington at the age of 84. Not a bad age considering he wasn't expected to survive past the first day of his life. Newton died a wealthy man and was one of the most famous men in England. His discoveries helped change the world – the legacy Newton left behind was vast. Isaac Newton, who had once said: 'If I have seen further, it is by standing on the shoulders of giants', was buried in Westminster Abbey and was the first scientist to be buried there.

OLDEST IN ENGLAND

1. The oldest iron bridge in England is Tickford Bridge in Buckinghamshire. The bridge was built in 1810.

2. The oldest football club in England is Notts County Football Club in Nottingham which was formed in 1862.

3. England's oldest city is Ripon in Yorkshire. Alfred the Great granted it a charter in 886.

4. The Dunmow Flitch is the oldest recorded competition in England. It was first held in 1244. To win the prize, couples – who had been married for a year and a day – had to convince the judges that they had not once, sleeping or waking, regretted their marriage. The prize was a side of pork.

5. Greensted church in Essex is the oldest wooden church in England. The church is made from oak and has been standing there for nearly 1200 years.

6. The oldest Christian church in England is St Piran's Oratory, south of Newquay. It was built in the sixth century.

7. Colchester is widely believed to be England's oldest recorded town because it was mentioned by the Roman writer, Pliny the Elder, in his *Historia Naturalis* in AD 77.

8. 'The Oldest Sweet Shop in England' is in Pately Bridge, North Yorkshire. It was established in 1827. The family-run business has over 200 glass jars containing favourite varieties of sweets.

9. Saint Martin's Church in Canterbury is the oldest church in England still in use.

10. Chester Racecourse (known as Roodee) is the oldest racecourse still in use in England. Horse-racing in Chester dates back to the early 16th century.

11. England's oldest weekly magazine for women is *The Lady*. It began publication in 1885.

12. England's oldest cricket ground is Lord's Cricket Ground, London.

13. 'Ye Olde Fighting Cocks' in St Albans is thought to be England's oldest pub. It dates back to 795.

14. The oldest charitable institution in England is the 'Hospital of St Cross and Almshouse of Noble Poverty' in Winchester. The hospital, which is England's oldest continuing almshouse, was founded between 1133 and 1136.

15. Kent is England's oldest county.

16. 'Robert Reavley, Pharmaceutical Chemist' in Burford, Oxfordshire is England's oldest pharmacy still in operation. It has been a pharmacy under several ownerships since 1734.

17. Derby's Arboretum is said to be England's oldest public park. It was given to the city by local benefactor, Joseph Strutt, in 1840.

18. Opened in 1909, the 'Electric Cinema' in Birmingham is believed to be England's oldest working cinema.

19. England's oldest known timber-framed shop is in Berkhamsted High Street in Hertfordshire. It is said to be 700 years old.

20. Cheltham's Library in Manchester is England's oldest surviving public library. The library, where Karl Marx researched *Das Kapital*, was founded in 1653.

21. The Ashmolean Museum in Oxford, is England's oldest public museum. It dates back to 1683.

22. Jacka's bakery in Plymouth is England's oldest commercial bakery. It was established in 1597.

23. Oxford University is England's oldest university, dating back to the 11th century.

24. Old Hall Hotel in Buxton is reputed to be the oldest purpose built hotel in England. It was built in 1220.

OLYMPIC GAMES

The first modern Olympic Games were held in Chipping Camden in Gloucestershire in 1612 when Robert Dover held his 'Cotswold Olimpick Games'. The Games included events such as sledgehammer throwing, wrestling and horse-racing.

PARLIAMENTARY PROCEEDINGS

Since the reign of Edward VI (1537-1553), the English Parliament has kept a daily record – the *Journal* – of all that has happened within its walls. Before the existence of the *Journal*, details of parliamentary proceedings were kept in the *Rolls of Parliament* – and written in Latin. In the first 200 years of its existence, the *Journal* varied in style according to the whims of the person keeping it. Sometimes the clerk simply noted the Bills and Motions before the House. In early Stuart days, fragments of speeches were recorded in the *Journal* alongside notes recording strange incidents. By the 18th century, the *Journal* had become more dignified. Today, the official records of parliamentary proceedings are kept in *Hansard*.

The excerpts which follow, taken from the *Journal* and the *Rolls of Parliament*, are revealing.

(The earliest of these entries, which appeared in the *Rolls of Parliament*, carry only the year of their inclusion.)

1. 'Whereas after the laws of this land, no person should use any unlawful games – as Dice, Quoits, Football and such like games – but every person fit and able in body ought to be able to use his bow, because the defence of this land standeth in need of archers.' (*1477*)

2. 'That no manner of person under the estate of a Lord, shall wear any gown or cloak, except it be of such length it, he being upright, shall cover his privy members and buttocks.' (*1482*)

3. 'Francis Drake, Esquire, is licensed this day by Mr Speaker to depart for certain his necessary business, in the service of her Majesty.' (*17 February 1580*)

4. 'A strange spaniel, of mouse-colour, came into the House.' (*14 May 1605*)

5. 'Long arguments upon the Bill...whether the Wednesday shall be a Fish-day. And upon the question, the House was divided; and they to have it a Fish-day were 179; and to have it not a Fish-day, were 97.' (*11 March 1622*)

6. 'Resolved, That the House will adjourn for Christmas Eve and Christmas Day only.' (*11 December 1648*)

7. 'Resolved, That in case any married woman shall be carnally known by any man other than her husband, except in case of ravishment...every such offence shall be and is hereby adjudged felony, and every person, as well the man as the woman, shall suffer death, as in case of felony, without benefit of clergy.' (*12 April 1650*)

8. 'Ordered, That an Act against the vice of Painting, and wearing black Patches, and immodest dress of women, be read on Friday morning next.' (*7 June 1650*)

9. 'Serjeant Wylde stood up to speak. Some moved that he had spoken, but leave was asked for him to speak, till the House was full. He mumbled on, and cited a great many cases. It seems, in the time of the Long Parliament, he was always left speaking, and members went to dinner, and found him speaking when they came in again.' (*18 March 1658*)

10. 'Mr Prynne (the MP for Bath) brought in this Bill, which was generally disliked and said to be full of dirty language.' (*24 September 1666*)

11. 'The House being informed, That there was a discourse of blowing up the two Houses of Parliament, and that this was the day for executing the same; Ordered That Sir Trevor Williams (and five others) do go and search the rooms underneath this House.' (*28 October 1678*)

12. 'Col Birch: 'I am in a new periwig, and pray let the House look at me before I am heard.' *(6 November 1689)*

13. 'A Bill for prohibiting the use of all Lotteries was read the second time.' (*1 February 1692*)

14. 'From Fees and Salaries payable at the Exchequer:

> Master of the Harriers £500.0.0
> Master of the Studs £200.0.0
> Master of the Hawks £1,372.10
> Clerk of the House of Commons: £10.0.0
> (*21 February 1694*)

15. 'Ordered, That leave be given to bring in a Bill to prevent mischief by squibs and other fireworks.' (*15 December 1697*)

16. 'Ordered, That leave be given to bring in a Bill to abolish trials by

single combat and to prevent the impious practice of Duelling.' (*11 April 1713*)

17. 'An ingrossed Bill, That all proceedings in Courts of Justice shall be in the English language, was read the Third time...and passed.' (*24 April 1731*)

18. 'A Petition of the Writing-Masters...setting forth, that notwithstanding the Act made in the 5th year of Elizabeth, numberds of mechanicks and other ignorant persons, intrude themselves into the profession, and pretend to teach the Arts of Writing and Bookkeeping, without the title of a severn years' apprenticeship, or any qualification for the same, to the great discouragement of the petitioners, and detriment of the publick.' (*25 February 1731*)

19. 'Petition of William Hogarth, George Vertue, and others, artists and designers of paintings, drawings, and engravers of original prints, alleging, That the Petitioners have, with great industry and expense, severally invented designed or engraved divers sets of new pictures and prints, in hopes to have reaped the benefits of such their own labours, and the credit thereof, but that divers printsellers, printers, and other persons, both here and abroad, have, of late, too frequently taken the liberty of copying, printing, publishing, great quantities of base, imperfect and mean copies and imitations thereof, to the great detriment of the petitioners and such other artists, and to the discouragement of Arts and Sciences in this Kingdom.' (*7 February 1734*)

20. 'Complaint made to the House, That great numbers of idle and disorderly persons to daily, under the pretence of asking for charity, infest the public streets and places of the City and Liberty of Westminster, to the great annoyance and interruption of members of this House in their passage to and from this House.' (*8 February 1739*)

21. 'Resolved, That the separation of the Corporation of Barbers and Surgeons, and making two corporations of the present united company of barbers and surgeons, will contribute much to the improvement of surgery, and thereby become a matter of public utility.' (*27 February 1744*)

22. 'And be it further enacted...That from and after the first day of August, 1747, no man or boy within that part of Great Britain called Scotland, other than such as shall be employed as officers or soldiers in HM Forces, shall, on any pretence whatsoever, wear or put on the clothes commonly called Highland clothes, that is to say, the plaid, philibeg or little kilt, trouse, shoulder-belts or any part whatsoever of what peculiarly belongs to the Highland garb.' (*1745*)

23. 'Resolved, That there shall be paid for every window, or light, in every dwelling house inhabited within the kingdom of Great Britain, which shall contain ten windows or lights, and less than fifteen, the yearly sum of sixpence and in every dwelling house as aforesaid, which shall contain fifteen windows or lights, and less than twenty, the yearly sum of ninepence for each window, or light, in such house; and in every dwelling house, as aforesaid, which shall contain twenty windows or lights, or upwards, the yearly sum of one shilling for each window or light, in such house. (*January 1746*)

24. 'Ordered, That a Committee be appointed to inquire into the state of the private madhouses in this kingdom.' (*27 January 1762*)

25. 'Ordered, That leave be given to bring in a Bill for the regulation of private madhouses in this kingdom.' (*22 February 1762*)

26. 'Mr Serjeant Glynn was suffering under a severe attack of the gout. He was brought down in a sedan, and carried to his seat in the House by two servants.' (*15 April 1769*)

27. 'Resolved, That the same duty be laid on all feather beds imported into this Kingdom as are payable upon the importation of feathers for beds.' (*1 April 1776*)

28. 'The total number of inhabited and uninhabited

    Houses: 701,473,
    Cottages: 243,901
    Others: 7,360
    Total: 952,734
    (*9 March 1778*)

29. 'Such a snow as has not been known in the memory of man came

on, which not only covered the earth in the space of an hour, that would have rendered it almost impossible to travel, but so filled the hemisphere as to render it altogether impossible to do so, for it so thickened the air that a man sitting on horseback could not discern his horse's head, and therefore he could not get back to Lewes that night, but remained at Eastbourne, and the next morning as soon as it was light, set out with a guide and after being buried many times with his horse in the snow, and at the utmost hazard of his life, reached Lewes so that the said petition could not reach the House until after it was risen.' (*1 February 1781*)

30. 'The committee recommends duties on candles, bricks, tiles, felt hats, horses, silk handkerchiefs, linen, ribbons, gauze and that licences be charged to selling mead, brandy, beer, wine, vinegar, hops and candles.' (*1 July 1784*)

31. 'Petition from the Proprietors and Farmers in Northumberland, Durham, Berwick and Roxbury Complaining of the mischiefs arising from the great number of useless and unnecessary dogs, And praying, That a general, uniform and annual Tax be laid upon all dogs without exception; and if the money a rising be not wanted for other purposes of state, that it may be applied as a Fund for maintaining the poor in each county, or lessen the duties on soap, salt, candles and other necessities.' (*16 August 1784*)

32. 'A plan has been formed, by my direction, for transporting a number of convicts, in order to remove the inconveniences which arise from the crowded state of the gaols in different parts of the kingdom.' (23 January 1787 (from the King's Speech))

33. 'Receipts: £16,030,286

    Expenditure: £15,969,178
    Balance: £61,108
    (*10 May 1791*)

34. 'Ordered, That leave be given to bring in a Bill for vesting in Joseph Bramah his executors, administrators and assigns, the sole use and property of his invention of a new kind of lock for doors, drawers and other purposes.' (21 March 1798)

35. 'Naval Estimates: Chatham: Victory. 100 guns. Middling Repair.

To be taken in hand February 1799. To be completed December 1799. Cost £13,500.' (*26 November 1798*)

36. 'The member for Sussex, Mr Fuller, entered the House in a state of inebriety, and too audibly mistook the Speaker for an owl in an ivy-bush. He was at once named, and handed over to the Serjeant. The next day the Speaker administered a severe but dignified rebuke.' (*1810*)

PARLIAMENT – STATE OPENING

At the annual State Opening of Parliament, the Monarch delivers a speech (written for her by the ruling political party) in which she lists the measures 'her' Government intends to introduce during the coming session of Parliament.

When the Monarch is ready to deliver his or her speech in the House of Lords, an official employed by the Lords, known as 'Black Rod', is dispatched to the House of Commons to summon MPs to hear the Monarch's speech.

As Black Rod approaches the entrance to the Commons chamber, the door is slammed in his face to show the independence of the Commons from the Sovereign. With his rod, Black Rod bangs three times on the door. The door to the Commons chamber is then opened, Black Rod enters, bows respectfully and informs the MPs that they are needed at the House of Lords. The MPs then follow Black Rod to the House of Lords to hear the Monarch's speech.

PATRIOTISM

Two dozen great quotes about England:

1. 'There is a forgotten, nay almost forbidden, word which means more to me than any other. That word is England.' (*Winston Churchill*)

2. 'Remember that you are an Englishman, and consequently won first prize in the lottery of life.' (*Cecil Rhodes*)

3. 'When a man is tired of London, he is tired of life; for there is in London all that life can afford...' (*Samuel Johnson*)

4. 'If I should die, think only this of me: That there's some corner of a foreign field that is forever England.' (*Rupert Brooke*)

5. 'This blessed plot, this earth, this realm, this England.' (*William Shakespeare*)

6. 'England is perhaps the only great country whose intellectuals are ashamed of their own nationality. In left-wing circles it is always felt that there is something slightly disgraceful in being an Englishman and that it is a duty to snigger at every English institution, from horse-racing to suet puddings. It is a strange fact, but it is unquestionably true that almost any English intellectual would feel more ashamed of standing to attention during 'God Save the King' than of stealing from a poor box.' (*George Orwell*)

7. 'Like all other modern people, the English are in process of being numbered, labelled, conscripted, 'coordinated'. But the pull of their impulses is in the other direction, and the kind of regimentation that can be imposed on them will be modified in consequence.' (*George Orwell*)

8. 'Propose to any Englishman any principle, or any instrument, however admirable, and you will observe that the whole effort of the English mind is directed to find a difficulty, defect or an impossibility in it.' (*Charles Babbage*)

9. 'It was England that invented the forms of liberty that free people now call freedom.' (*Financial Times*)

10. 'They do not believe that there are any other people than themselves, or any other world than England: and whenever they see some handsome foreigner, they say, 'He looks like an Englishman,' or, 'What a pity he is not English.' (*Andrea Travisana, Venetian Ambassador, visiting London in 1497*)

11. 'The English people will go so far and then they get up on their stubborn hind legs.' (*Rafael Sabatini*)

12. 'God is an Englishman.' (*King Philip of Spain 1588*)

13. 'If it be true that nations have the cats they deserve, then the English people deserve well of cats, for there are none so prosperous or so friendly in the world.' (*Hilaire Belloc*)

14. 'Whatever else, I have been blessed with God's two greatest gifts: to be born English and heterosexual.' (*John Osborne*)

15. 'If an Englishman says there's no hurry, that means it must be done immediately. If he says he doesn't mind, it means he minds very much. If he leaves any decision to you by saying 'If you like' or 'When you like', be on your guard – he means that he's made his requirements clear, and he expects them to be precisely met.' (*Len Deighton*)

16. 'England expects that every man will do his duty.' (*Lord Horatio Nelson's message to his men, before the Battle of Trafalgar*)

17. 'England is the mother of parliaments.' (*John Bright*)

18. 'We the English seem, as it were, to have conquered and peopled half the world in a fit of absence of mind.' (*Sir John Robert Seeley*)

19. 'The best thing I know between France and England is – the sea.' (*Douglas William Jerrold*)

20. 'Smile at us, pay us, pass us; but do not quite forget. For we are the people of England, that never have spoken yet.' (*G. K. Chesterton*)

21. 'The Almighty in His infinite wisdom did not see fit to create Frenchmen in the image of Englishmen.' (*Winston Churchill*)

22. '...to be an Englishman is to belong to the most exclusive club there is.' (*Ogden Nash*)

23. 'The English are moral, the English are good. And clever, and modest, and misunderstood.' *(Michael Flanders)*

24. 'To eat well in England you should have breakfast three times a day.' (*Somerset Maugham*)

PETTY, WILLIAM (1623-1687)

William Petty was an inventor, a doctor, a surveyor and a businessman. He was also a statistician and economist and the originator of something he called 'political arithmetic' – which he defined as 'the art of reasoning by figures upon things relating to government'. (Petty himself was, for a while, a Member of Parliament.) He based his new economic theory on the work of Francis Bacon, who had argued that all rational sciences should be based on mathematics and the senses. Petty announced that his work would use only measurable phenomena and would rely on quantitative precision. His work on 'political arithmetic' was the foundation for modern census techniques.

In 1662, the year after he was knighted, Petty wrote *Treatise of Taxes and Contributions* in which he explained why he believed it was important to give free rein to 'the forces of individual self-interest'. He also declared that it was a duty of the State to maintain a high level of employment, and argued that a strong labour force makes a strong nation and a strong currency. He coined the term 'full employment'. This, and other subsequent books, were the foundation of economics.

Petty recommended that taxes should just be high enough to pay for providing support for the elderly, the sick and for orphans and that government expenditure in other areas should be kept to a minimum. He recommended that imports should be taxed, but only to put them on a par with domestic produce. He favoured taxes on consumption rather than income and recommended collecting statistical information in order to find ways to raise taxes more fairly.

Petty introduced precision into national accounting. He worked out that the average income in England at the time was £6 13 shillings and 6 pence per annum and that, with a population of six million, that meant a national income of £40 million.

Petty warned that governments should not over-interfere in the economy. He introduced the concept of 'laissez-faire' government and pointed out that it was as dangerous for a government to over-interfere with the economy as it would be for a physician to over-treat a patient. His *Essays in Political Arithmetick* and *Political Survey of Anatomy of Ireland* included calculated estimates of population and social income. Perhaps the greatest contribution Petty made was to base his theories on data and statistics rather than on anecdotal evidence and prejudice. He was a prolific author on economics but wrote precisely and with humour. His work greatly influenced every writer on economics who followed him – particularly, for example, Adam Smith and Karl Marx. Adam Smith knew of Petty's work but does not credit him as the originator of his own ideas on the economy. Smith's derivative book *Inquiry into the Nature and Causes of the Wealth of Nations*, was not published until 1776, over a century after Petty had written his masterpiece *Treatise on Taxes and Contributions*. It was Englishman William Petty, not Scotsman Adam Smith, who invented many of the concepts that are still used in economics today.

PHOTOGRAPHY

William Henry Fox Talbot (1800-1877) the squire of Lacock of Wiltshire, invented photography. He began the researches which led to the invention of photography in 1826, but it was his hobby of drawing which eventually led to photography. In 1833, while on his honeymoon near Lake Como in Italy, Talbot was tracing over the images produced through a 'camera obscura' when he decided he wanted to find a way to make such images permanent. Two years later, in 1835, he invented the paper negative and in 1840 he invented the calotype, or talbotype, an early photographic process which involved the use of a photographic negative from which multiple prints could be made. Talbot started taking photographs in that year and the oldest photographic negative in existence in the world is an image of a latticed window in his home, Lacock Abbey, which was taken in 1835. In 1844, Talbot published *The Pencil of Nature*, the first book in the world to be illustrated with photographs

PIERS

Half a dozen of the longest seaside piers in England:

1. Southend-on-Sea, Essex – 7,080 feet
2. Southport, Lancashire – 3,633 feet
3. Walton-on-the-Naze, Essex – 2,600 feet
4. Ryde, Isle of Wight – 2,305 feet

5. Hythe, Hampshire – 2,100 feet

6. Brighton Palace, East Sussex – 1,760 feet

PIRATES

The Most Successful English Pirates

1. Sir Francis Drake

Born in Plymouth, Drake was a pirate from 1572 to 1596. Officially commissioned as a pirate by Queen Elizabeth I (who knighted him in 1581 and called him 'her pirate'). He made a fortune from captured Spanish galleons. He worked in the Caribbean and east Pacific, and sailed in a ship called the Golden Hind.

2. Edward Teach

Known as Blackbeard, because he had a black beard, Edward Teach was born in Bristol and worked as a pirate from 1716 to 1718. He operated in the Caribbean and off the east coast of America. He is famous for his long black beard and for routinely carrying two swords, six pistols and a variety of knives. (He would have enormous difficulty getting through customs these days.) His favourite drink was rum laced with gunpowder and to make himself look frightening (as though the armaments weren't enough) he wore lighted lengths of cord in his hair.

3. Sir Christopher Myngs

Born in Norfolk, Myngs worked as a pirate from 1656 to 1665 in the Caribbean. He was made a vice-admiral in the English navy when he returned home.

4. William Dampier

Born near Yeovil in Somerset and worked as a pirate in the Atlantic, the Pacific, the South China seas and the Caribeean. He operated from 1679 to 1715.

5. Henry Every

Known as Long Ben though no one could remember why, was

born in Plymouth and operated as a pirate in the Indian Ocean from 1694 to 1696.

6. Sir John Hawkins
Born in Plymouth, like so many pirates, Hawkins worked as a pirate in the Caribbean from 1562 to 1595. He was given his ship by Queen Elizabeth I and knighted for helping to defeat the Spanish Armada.

7. Mary Read
There weren't many female pirates but Mary Read was hugely successful. She was born in London, worked in the Caribbean as a pirate from 1719 to 1720 and fought as a man in both the army and the navy before becoming a pirate. She took part in boarding parties and fought duels. She is reputed to have won a duel with another pirate by suddenly baring her breasts and then decapitating him as he stared in astonishment.

8. Edward Low
Low, born in London, worked in the Caribbean, the Azores and the east coast of north America from 1721 to 1724. He cut the lips from one member of his crew and forced the man to watch him fry them. And he chopped off the ears of a captive and made him eat them. Perhaps not surprisingly, he was set adrift in a small boat by mutineers.

NAMES OF PLACES
The Meanings of Three Dozen English Place Names

1. Aldringham (Suffolk) – 'Homestead of the family or followers of a man called Aldhere'.
2. Bagshot (Surrey) – 'Projecting piece of land frequented by badgers'.
3. Basingstoke (Hampshire) – 'Secondary settlement or outlying farmstead of the family or followers of a man called Basa'.
4. Calverleigh (Devon) – 'Clearing in the bare wood'.

5. Catmore (W. Berks.) – 'Pool frequented by wild-cats'.

6. Dishforth (N. Yorks.) – 'Ford across a ditch'.

7. Dunster (Somerset) – 'Craggy hill-top of a man called Dun(n).

8. Edgbaston (Birmingham) – 'Farmstead of a man called Ecgbald'.

9. Elstead (Surrey) – 'Place where elder trees grow'.

10. Faulkbourne (Essex) – 'Stream frequented by falcons'.

11. Finchley (Gtr. London) – 'Woodland clearing frequented by finches'.

12. Gatwick (W. Sussex) – 'Farm where goats are kept'.

13. Gumley (Leics.) – 'Woodland clearing of a man called Godmund'.

14. Hawkhurst (Kent) – 'Wooded hill frequented by hawks'.

15. Horsington (Somerset) – 'Farmstead of the horsekeepers or grooms'.

16. Ide Hill (Kent) – 'Hill of a woman called Edith'.

17. Kepwick (N. Yorks) – 'Hamlet with a market'.

18. Kersey (Suffolk) – 'Island where cress grows'.

19. Littlemore (Oxon) – 'Little Marsh'.

20. Marlow (Bucks.) – 'Land remaining after the draining of a pool'.

21. Nutfield (Surrey) – 'Open land where nut trees grow'.

22. Penzance (Cornwall) – 'Holy Headland'.

23. Podmore (Staffs) – 'Marsh frequented by toads or frogs'.

24. Rampton (Cambs.) – 'Farmstead where rams are kept'.

25. Riverhead (Kent) – 'Landing place for cattle'.

26. Salford (Oxon) – 'Ford over which salt is carried'.

27. Shoreditch (Gtr. London) – 'Ditch leading to the riverbank (of the Thames)'.

28. Sidmouth (Devon) – 'Mouth of the River Sid'.

29. Thursford (Norfolk) – 'Ford associated with a giant or demon'.

30. Tollerton (N. Yorks) – 'Farmstead or village of the tax-gatherers'.
31. Tolpuddle (Dorset) – 'Estate on the River Piddle belonging to a woman called Tóla'.
32. Whenby (N. Yorks) – 'Farmstead or village of the women'.
33. Wonersh (Surrey) – 'Crooked ploughed field'.
34. Wormley (Herts) – 'Woodland clearing infested with snakes'.
35. Ullock (Cumbria) – 'Place where wolves play'.
36. Yarnfield (Staffs) – 'Open land frequented by eagles'.

PLOUGHMAN'S LUNCH

A ploughman's lunch is the quintessential English pub lunch. Every pub chef will have his or her own version of what the Ploughman's Lunch should be, but the traditional ingredients are usually a large piece of crusty bread, lots of butter, a big slice of cheese (usually cheddar) and some pickles. The pickles may include pickled onions or the more popular choice Branston pickle. Chutney or piccalilli may also be used. Ploughman's Lunch is often served with lots of crispy, green salad, though this is a modern, rather fancy addition and not traditional.

POPE ADRIAN IV

Pope Adrian IV was born Nicholas Breakspear in around 1100 in Abbot's Langley, near St Albans in Hertfordshire. He was the only Englishman ever to hold the office of Pope. He was Pope for just five years, from 1154 to 1159, and his policies caused political chaos throughout Europe.

Pope Adrian IV is famous for two things. In 1155, he withdrew the sacraments from the people and suspended public worship in Rome after a cardinal was killed during a riot. And he published a bull called Laudabiliter which gave dominion over Ireland to Henry II of England for his lifetime. (The 'for his lifetime' bit was ignored by Henry's heirs and the gift caused some small degree of lasting disagreement between the English and the Irish.)

POUND

The pound (the English currency) gets its name from the fact that the unit of currency was originally based on the value of a troy pound weight of high purity silver.

The £ symbol is based on a traditional capital L with a horizontal line through it, and is derived from the Latin word libra.

The word 'sterling' dates back to the reign of Henry II in the 12th century. Sterling silver's hallmark used to feature a starling – and the word was probably corrupted and ended up as 'sterling'.

An alternative explanation is that the word sterling may be derived from the name 'Easterling silver', which refers to silver mined in an area of Germany of that name. Easterling was famous for the high quality of its silver and the metal was for many years imported into England to form the basis of the country's silver coins.

PUBS

There have been pubs in England since the Bronze Age. Travellers stopped at inns for refreshment when they were tired and thirsty after a day on the road. Locals found them a useful meeting place.

By the 18th century, alcoholism had become a major problem in England. This was largely due to the introduction of gin which was cheap and readily available in gin-shops. By 1740, drinkers were getting through six times as much gin as beer. (The problems of alcoholism were illustrated by William Hogarth in a famous series of engravings entitled 'Beer Street and Gin Lane'.)

By the early 1800s, there were so many gin houses (or gin palaces as they were sometimes known) that alcoholism and crime had become serious national problems.

The Government's response was to introduce the Beer Act of 1830. The plan was to persuade drinkers to switch from gin to beer by increasing the number of available shops where beer could be bought. At the time, medical experts regarded beer as nutritious and harmless. Young children were often given 'small beer' (a relatively low alcohol content drink) because it was considered safer for them to drink beer than to drink the water.

Under the Act of 1830, any householder could pay a one off fee of two guineas for a licence to sell beer in his own home. The licence even entitled householders to brew their own beer in their own homes. The beer house proprietors were only allowed to sell beer and if they were caught selling spirits or wine they were fined and closed down.

The people running these beer houses made huge amounts of money. They would start by selling beer in their front parlour and, when they'd made enough money, they would buy the house next door to live in and turn every room in their old house into a bar, a snug, a saloon or a lounge.

In the first year after the Beer Act came into operation, just 400 beer houses were opened. Within eight years there were 46,000 beer houses across England. The licence was cheap and the profits were huge. In some towns nearly every other house was a 'beer house'.

By 1869, the Government realised that it had made a mistake. New stricter licensing laws were introduced. But the beer houses which were already in existence were allowed to continue and a good many of them applied for full licences so that they could sell wine and spirits in addition to beer.

All this explains why so many towns have pubs situated right in the middle of a street of ordinary looking houses. The pubs which are so situated probably began their lives as 'beer houses' and were turned into fully-fledged public houses as the years went by.

PUB NAMES (POPULAR)

Here are the most popular names for English pubs:

1. Red Lion
2. Royal Oak

3. Railway
4. Crown
5. White Hart
6. New Inn
7. Bell
8. Swan
9. Plough
10. King's Head
11. Kings Arms
12. White Horse

PUB NAMES (STRANGE)

England has a good many curiously named pubs. Here are a dozen of the oddest we've spotted:

1. The Bucket of Blood – Cornwall
2. The Bishops Finger – Canterbury, Kent
3. The Roaring Donkey – Swindon, Wiltshire
4. The Bunch of Carrots – Hampton Bishop, Hereford
5. Ferret & Radiator – Dawlish, Devon
6. The Who'd a Thowt It – Middleton, Manchester
7. Nobody Inn – Doddiscombsleigh, Devon
8. The Flying Handbag – Blackpool
9. The Jolly Taxpayer – Plymouth
10. Flying Saucer – Gillingham, Kent
11. Gay Dog Inn – Earls Croome, Worcestershire
12. Goat & Tricycle – Bournemouth, Dorset

PUDDINGS

Puddings are a mainstay of the English diet. Unlike 'sweets' which usually consist of delicate confections such as meringue and ice cream, puddings are stodgy, filling and served hot. Here are a dozen traditional English puddings:

1. Spotted Dick *(See Spotted Dick)*
2. Bread and Butter Pudding *(See Bread and Butter Pudding)*
3. Treacle Sponge Pudding
4. Sticky Toffee Pudding
5. Rhubarb Crumble
6. Jam Roly Poly
7. Cabinet Pudding
8. Apple Charlotte
9. Cherry Pie
10. Lemon Meringue Pie
11. Sussex Pond Pudding
12. Christmas Pudding

PUNCH AND JUDY

With his hooked nose, jutting chin and famous catchphrase, 'That's the way to do it!' Mr Punch is a very recognisable English character. The Punch and Judy puppets are husband and wife and used to be very popular in England. Their red and white striped show tents can still sometimes be seen around English seaside resorts during the summer months but political correctness has caused their decline in recent years. Here are half a dozen facts about Punch and Judy:

1. An early version of the Punch puppet was first recorded in Samuel Pepys's Diary on May 9th 1662. This date is now the official birthdate of Mr Punch.

2. Mr Punch was originally a stringed puppet.

3. Mr Punch's wife, Judy, used to be called Joan.

4. The phrase, 'as pleased as punch' came about as a result of Mr Punch.

5. The main characters in the Punch and Judy show include: Mr Punch, his wife Judy, their baby, a crocodile, a policeman, a doctor, a ghost and Joey the clown.

6. The Punch and Judy man (the puppeteer) is called a professor. The puppeteer holds a device called a 'swazzle' in his mouth to create Mr Punch's rasping voice.

QUEUES

The English like nothing better than a good queue. You only have to go to the shops around the festive season to see hour-long orderly queues formed of calm, obedient customers buying presents for their loved ones. Some people will even happily queue all night if there's a January sale on at their local department store.

Here are the rules of etiquette for queuing:

1. Do not push in; this is very much frowned upon in England. Not only is it rude but it is also disrespectful to the others in the queue. You will almost certainly be told, politely but firmly, to get to the end of the queue. As you do your walk of shame, you will see much glaring in your direction and shaking of heads from the other people in the queue.

2. If you reach the queue at the same time as someone else, it is considered good etiquette to allow him or her to go first.

3. Do not chew gum, talk on your mobile, whistle or hum loudly whilst queuing. Queuing should be taken seriously and done quietly.

4. Do not stand too close to the person in front of you; each of us needs his or her personal space.

5. If you know you're about to cough or sneeze, then please put your hand over your mouth. There is nothing worse than a wet sneeze landing on the back of your neck.

6. After having finished at the till, stand aside. This allows the next person in line to come to the till while you sort out your change.

RALEGH, WALTER (1552-1618)
(ALSO SPELT RALEIGH)

Walter Ralegh was a sailor, adventurer, pirate, poet, soldier, courtier, explorer and entrepreneur. He was one of England's great 16th century heroes. Today he is remembered for laying down his cloak so that Queen Elizabeth I didn't have to step in a puddle.

The story that Ralegh won the Queen's affection by laying down his cloak for her first appeared in a book called *Worthies* written in 1662 by Fuller. 'Captain Raleigh coming out of Ireland to the English court in good habit found the Queen walking, till meeting with a plashy place, she seemed to scruple going thereon. Presently Raleigh cast and spread his new plush cloak on the ground; whereon the Queen trod gently, rewarding him afterwards with many suits, for his so free and seasonable tender of so fair a foot cloth.' Thus Ralegh became a favourite of the Queen and a puddle became a legend.

Ralegh travelled the world. He discovered 'Virginia' and named it after the Virgin Queen of England. He acted as an officially appointed pirate, and acquired a huge fortune in gold. He introduced tobacco and potatoes to England. He took part in the defeat of the Spanish Armada, and he wrote books about his travels.

When Elizabeth died, Ralegh knew little of the new monarch, King James I. He had failed to win over the new King (the cloak and puddle trick doesn't work as well with a King as it does with a Queen) and his position at court quickly became insecure. He was falsely accused of trying to assassinate the King. Desperate, he tried to commit suicide. This was regarded as a sign of guilt. He was tried in Winchester and condemned to a traitor's death. He was kept a prisoner in the Tower of London for 13 years (though he was allowed one final voyage across the Atlantic before being executed). While in prison, his wife and sons were allowed to stay with him and he was allowed to build a laboratory where he carried out a series of chemical experiments. He managed to obtain fresh water from salt water and created several new drugs. And he wrote an ambitious *History of the World*, using his library of six or seven hundred volumes for source material.

Walter Ralegh was a courageous, resourceful and versatile Englishman. He was a soldier, sailor, author, poet, traveller and coloniser. He was a philosopher, a politician and a historian. He acquired a fortune but was not afraid to use it when he needed it.

Walter Ralegh was a man of his time; a great romantic, a great hero, a great Englishman.

After Ralegh was beheaded, his wife Elizabeth had his head embalmed and kept it in a red leather bag by her side for the rest of her life.

REBELS AND REVOLUTIONARIES

A dozen Englishmen who had the courage of their convictions (and were often convicted for their courage):

1. Stephen Langton
2. Oliver Cromwell
3. William Cobbett
4. Thomas Paine
5. Daniel Defoe
6. Wat Tyler
7. John Lilburne
8. John Locke
9. Thomas More
10. William Tyndale
11. John Wycliffe
12. John Wilkes

RENAISSANCE

Italy may have led the renaissance in the 14th and 15th centuries but it was England which took over in the 16th century with Shakespeare, Sidney, Bacon, Ralegh, Spenser and More. The industrial revolution began in England and from then on England led the world in almost every conceivable branch of exploration, science and literature.

ROGET, PETER MARK (1779-1869)

The modern thesaurus was invented by, and is named after, Peter Mark Roget. Roget was born in London and he qualified and worked as a physician.

In 1840, Roget retired from medical work to concentrate on the most notable work of his life. This was, of course, his *Thesaurus of English Words and Phrases*, a most comprehensive and classified collection of synonyms which enables writers to find an alternative word when they are creating a letter, an article or a book and do not wish to keep repeating themselves. Roget was the first person to create a thesaurus. He had always loved lists and had something of an obsession for list making when he was eight years old.

He started work on the thesaurus in 1805 and it was, for him, a way of escaping from depression. The book was first published in 1852 when it was given the snappy title: *Thesaurus of English Words and Phrases Classified and Arranged so as to Facilitate the Expression of Ideas and Assist in Literary Composition*. The book was reprinted 28 times during Roget's life. After Roget died, his son, John Lewis Roget, took over the job of keeping the book up-to-date. And when he, in turn, died, his son, Samuel Romilly Roget carried on the family tradition.

ROLLS ROYCE
Half a Dozen Facts

1. Henry Royce was born in 1883 in Alwalton in Huntingdonshire. His parents didn't have much money, so Henry decided to move to London to make his 'fortune'. His first job in London was delivering newspapers for W.H. Smith.

2. While working in London, Royce attended night school and studied electricity. When he had saved a little money he formed a company called F.H. Royce and Co. in Manchester. The company made electrical products and was successful. Royce spent some of his money on a second-hand French Decauville motor car. He thought he could do better. So he made a car.

3. In 1904, Henry Royce drove his two-cylinder car for the first time. He drove from Manchester to Knutsford. Royce made several more cars and improved upon the design each time.

4. Henry Royce's cars soon acquired a reputation for quality and innovation. Wealthy enthusiast, Charles Rolls, decided to make the journey from London to Manchester to have a look. Rolls was so impressed by what he saw that he decided to join forces with Henry Rolls. He wanted to 'sell the best car in the world'.

5. Rolls-Royce was formed in 1906, and that year the company made its first Rolls-Royce Silver Ghost car.

6. In 1910, Charles Rolls died in an aircraft accident. However, Royce remained head of the company and continued to make Rolls-Royce motor cars, designing each one, until his retirement in 1930. Royce died in 1933 and was buried in his home village, Alwalton. As a token of respect the badges on Rolls-Royce motor cars were changed from red to black.

ROSE

The rose is the national English flower. There are more than 30,000 varieties. Henry VII made the rose a royal emblem after the Wars of the Roses (between the House of Lanacaster and the House of York). He superimposed the red rose of Lancashire onto the white rose of York to symbolise the end of the hostilities.

ROUTH, JONATHAN (1927-2008)

Jonathan Routh, who was born in Gosport, Hampshire, was England's greatest ever prankster. Here are his best pranks (many of which were arranged for the TV series Candid Camera in which he starred in the 1960s.):

1. A car from which the engine had been removed coasted downhill and into a garage. The puzzled garage mechanic then struggled to find an engine.

2. A woman attempted to pack cakes on a conveyor belt that had been rigged to run three times as fast as usual.

3. Routh had himself posted as 'registered livestock' from Sheepwash in Devon to Fleet Street in London. He was accompanied on the journey by a postal official who remained politely silent throughout the journey.

4. He attempted to take a grand piano onto the London Underground.

5. He persuaded a crowd of tourists that Nelson's Column needed holding up.

6. He arranged a pyramid of plates in such a way that they crashed when anyone walked past them.

7. He asked a passer-by for tuppence for a cup of tea and, having got the money, produced a Thermos flask, milk and sugar, offered the cup of tea to the puzzled purchaser, asking if they wanted one lump, or two.

8. Routh rigged a mirror in a hat shop so that it cracked from side to side when anyone looked in it.

9. He was thrown out of Cambridge University for gathering hundreds of signatures for a campaign to stop an imaginary motorway being built across Bletchley Park.

10. He hid inside a postbox and talked to people as they posted letters.

11. He was ejected from Uppingham School for hanging a banner reading 'Vote Routh, Communist' in the school chapel.

12. He arranged for a public telephone kiosk to be lifted into the air as people made calls from it.

In later life, Routh became a professional painter. His work included paintings of Queen Victoria doing the hula-hoop and the limbo dance, riding a zebra and driving a dodgem car. He also painted the pope windsurfing and the Mona Lisa both naked and smoking.

ROYAL ENGLAND

Here are a dozen facts about the Kings and Queens of England:

1. George IV cut a lock of hair from every woman he slept with, and put each lock in a separate envelope. When he died, he was reported to have had 7,000 of these envelopes in his bedroom.

2. Queen Victoria's first language was German.

3. During King George III's phase of madness, he once mistook an oak tree for the King of Prussia.

4. Queen Elizabeth I never met Mary Queen of Scots, the cousin she had beheaded.

5. King Richard I (the Lionheart) only spent six months of his 10-year reign in England. He claimed it was 'cold and always raining'.

6. King Henry VIII was very musical and could play the organ, viola, virginal, lute and harp. He also composed songs (though he did not compose 'Greensleeves'). In his later years, King Henry VIII had a waist measurement of 54 inches.

7. King John suffered from seasickness. He found it so distressing that he hired a Royal Head Holder to hold his head steady when

he was at sea. The Royal Head Holder's name was Solomon Attefeld. Out of gratitude for Solomon's service, King John awarded him land.

8. King George I brought two mistresses to England with him when his wife Sophia was imprisoned for adultery. One of his mistresses was tall and skinny; the other mistress was short and fat. The public nicknamed the two mistresses: 'the Maypole and the Elephant'.

9. King Richard I's wife, Berengaria of Navarre, is the only English Queen never to have set foot in England.

10. Queen Anne, the last of the Stuart monarchs, had 17 pregnancies. Only one of her children survived infancy, but, sadly, even that one did not survive long enough to inherit the throne.

11. After King Charles I's execution his head was sewn back onto his body.

12. When Edward I lost his beloved wife, Queen Eleanor, he had a stone cross erected at every point he and the funeral cortege stayed during their journey to her funeral in London. The last stop being Charing Cross.

ROYAL RESIDENCES

Royal residences in England that are occupied by the Royal Family as family homes include:

1. Buckingam Palace (London)
2. Kensington Palace (London)
3. Sandringham House (Sandringham, Norfolk)
4. St James's Palace (London)
5. Windsor Castle (Windsor, Berkshire)

ROYAL QUOTES

1. 'Now nephew, to your work! Hey! St George for England!' (*King Charles II speaking to William of Orange on his wedding night*)

2. 'I am sorry, gentlemen, for being such a time a-dying.' (*King Charles II, apologising on his deathbed*)

3. 'There is no marvel in a woman learning to speak, but there would be in teaching her to hold her tongue.' (*Queen Elizabeth I replying to the French Ambassador after he had praised her ability to speak French.*)

4. 'I may not be a lion but I am a lion's cub, and I have a lion's heart.' (*Queen Elizabeth I*)

5. 'This Earle of Oxford (Edward de Vere, 17th earl, 1550-1604), making his low obeisance to Queen Elizabeth, happened to let a Fart, at which he was so abashed and ashamed that he went to Travell, 7 yeares. On his returne, the Queen welcomed him home, and sayd, 'My Lord, I had forgotten the Fart.' (*This anecdote about Queen Elizabeth I is taken from John Aubrey's classic 'Brief Lives' – first published 1813*)

6. 'I have already joined myself in marriage to a husband, namely the kingdom of England.' (*Elizabeth I, replying to critics who wanted her to get married.*)

SAINT GEORGE

According to a 5th century document, St George was put to death three times – by being chopped to pieces, buried deep in the earth and consumed by fire. Each time he was resurrected by the power of God. He vanquished dragons, destroyed armies and heathen idols, prompted wholesale conversions to Christianity and caused timber beams to burst into life. Despite the exaggerated legends about him, he almost certainly existed. In addition to being chopped up, buried and set alight he was also poisoned, stretched on the wheel and boiled alive. When, in desperation, his persecutors chopped off his head – milk rather than blood flowed from his head. In icons of Eastern Orthodox origin, George is seen spearing a dragon since the dragon is an ancient image for the Devil. George destroying the dragon is a symbol for Christianity overcoming the Devil, or good triumphing over evil. The legend was first published in detail in *The Golden Legend* published in English by William Caxton in 1483. It is said that a dragon which occupied marshland around the city of Selena in Libya could only be placated by being given human sacrifices. Victims were chosen by lot and on the day that Cleodolinda the King of Selena's daughter was chosen, St George, in full armour, happened to be riding by. After making the sign of the cross, George pinned the dragon to the ground with his lance and killed it with his sword. The King and all his subjects immediately converted to Christianity.

George is believed to have visited Glastonbury, and in 1061 a church was dedicated to him in Doncaster. Edward III made George the patron of the Order of the Garter and Richard I (Richard the Lionheart) made him the patron saint of soldiers for his Holy Crusades. In 1222, George was given a feast day (April 23 – which is coincidentally, regarded as Shakespeare's birthday) and by the end of the 14th century he was the patron saint of England. In 1415, his feast day was raised to equal status with Christmas. Shakespeare wrote about St George in Henry V's speech before the battle of Agincourt, and Edmund Spenser wrote about him in *The Faerie Queene*. Henry VIII decided that St George's cross should be the flag of the English navy and army. Later, James I crossed St George's flag with the blue cross of St Andrew to create the early Union Jack. In 1940, George VI created the George Cross for 'acts of the greatest heroism or of the most conspicuous courage in circumstances of extreme danger'. St George, killing the dragon, appears on one side of the medal. St George stands for all that is best in Englishness. He was modest and self-effacing, but valiant, patriotic, dutiful and upright. He fought fearlessly for right against wrong.

SANDWICH

The Earl of Sandwich invented the sandwich (he had been gambling all night and was peckish so ordered a piece of meat to be placed between two slices of bread so that he didn't have to leave the gaming table) and, thus, in one brief moment, which combined hunger and passion, created the world's fast food industry.

SCHOOLS

A number of English schools are more than 1,000 years old. The following are among the oldest schools in England (and, indeed, the world):

1. King's School Canterbury – Founded in AD 597
2. King's School Rochester – Founded in AD 604
3. St Peter's School, York – Founded AD 627
4. Warwick School – Founded AD 914
5. St Alban's School – Founded AD 948
6. King's School, Ely – Founded AD 970

SEASIDE

Buckets and spades, colourful plastic windmills, sand in your sandwiches, the sound of seagulls and the smell of the salt air. Oh, how we English do love to be beside the seaside. The following are a dozen of the most popular English seaside resorts:

1. Bournemouth (Dorset)
2. Great Yarmouth (Norfolk)
3. Eastbourne (Sussex)
4. Torquay (Devon)
5. Brighton (Sussex)
6. Newquay (Cornwall)
7. Blackpool (Lancashire)
8. Lyme Regis (Dorset)
9. Woolacombe (Devon)
10. Padstow (Cornwall)

11. Southend-on-Sea (Essex)

12. Weston-super-Mare (Somerset)

SHAKESPEARE, WILLIAM (1564-1616)

William Shakespeare, poet and playwright, and universally acknowledged as the greatest writer the world has ever seen, contributed more than any other individual to the English language.

If it were not for Shakespeare, many phrases in our English language today would simply not exist. His entire work contains between 25,000-30,000 different words (far, far more words than most writers use); some of these words were invented by Shakespeare, many were given new meanings by him. The following are a dozen facts about Shakespeare:

1. Shakespeare was born in a house on Henley Street, Stratford-on-Avon in 1564. He was one of seven children. Very little is known about his life but his parents were John Shakespeare and Mary Arden.

2. Shakespeare's father, John, was a big wheel in the small town of Stratford. He owned a profitable glove making business. In 1557 he joined the town council and in 1568, rose to the position of high bailiff.

3. In the 1570s, touring actors would frequently stop off at Stratford-on-Avon where they would perform plays. These plays no doubt made a strong impression on the growing Shakespeare, and probably sowed the seed for his future career in acting and writing.

4. In 1582, at the age of 18, William Shakespeare married Anne Hathaway who was eight years his senior. The couple had two daughters and a son: Susanna (who was the eldest) and twins, Judith and Hamnet. Sadly, Hamnet died in childhood. Little is known about what Shakespeare did for a living at this time but in the late 1580s he seems to have left his family and headed for London to seek his fortune. There is no documentary evidence

of what happened to him and these are often referred to as 'the lost years'. Little is known about his life because Shakespeare was a poor man with no university education, no contacts at court and no status.

5. In 1594, after having spent some years being involved in the theatre in London, Shakespeare became a member – and a shareholder – of a newly founded theatre company called 'The Lord Chamberlain's Men' (later named 'The King's Men' after King James I succeeded the throne).

6. As well as being a shareholder, William Shakespeare acted in the company and wrote plays for them to perform. Indeed, documents suggest that Shakespeare acted throughout his professional life.

7. Before he joined 'The Lord Chamberlain's Men', Shakespeare was already making a name for himself as a playwright; the first reference to him in this capacity was in 1592 and by 1596, Shakespeare had made enough money to buy a house called 'New Place' in Stratford-on-Avon for himself and his wife and children.

8. From 1599, Shakespeare's company of players performed at the Globe Theatre in London. Nearly all of Shakespeare's new plays were presented at the Globe, and he soon earned a reputation as one of England's greatest playwrights. His comedies include: *Love's Labour's Lost*, *The Taming of the Shrew*, *A Midsummer Night's Dream* and *The Comedy of Errors*. The history plays include: *Henry VI* (*Part I*, *II* and *III*), *Richard III* and *Richard II*. His tragedies include: *Romeo and Juliet*, *Hamlet*, *Othello*, *Julius Ceasar* and *Macbeth*. Nobody is really certain in what order many of his plays were written and first performed.

9. William Shakespeare wrote 37 plays and 154 sonnets. It is widely believed that Shakespeare's sonnets were printed without his consent, and one theory is that someone who knew Shakespeare betrayed him by handing his sonnets to a publisher.

10. William Shakespeare's plays are performed more often than those of any other playwright.

11. William Shakespeare died on April 23 1616. He was just 52-years-old. Nobody really knows for certain what caused his

death, though since he is believed to have had some sort of fever he probably died of an infection. Before he died, Shakespeare wrote his own epitaph of which the last line reads: 'And curst be he that moves my bones'.

12. In his will, Shakespeare left his wife, Anne, his second-best bed. However, this was not as bad as it seems, as the best bed around that period was usually reserved for guests, and the second bed was often the marital bed. Anne died seven years after her husband's death.

Shakespeare's England

From Act II Scene I, 'Richard II' by William Shakespeare

This royal throne of kings, this scepter'd isle,
This earth of majesty, this seat of Mars,
This other Eden, demi-paradise,
This fortress built by Nature for herself
Against infection and the hand of war,
This happy breed of men, this little world,
This precious stone set in the silver sea,
Which serves it in the office of a wall,
Or as a moat defensive to a house,
Against the envy of less happier lands,
This blessed plot, this earth, this realm, this England,
This nurse, this teeming womb of royal kings,
Fear'd by their breed and famous by their birth,
Renowned for their deed...Far from home,
For Christian service and true chivalry.

Shakespeare – Quotes from his plays

Here are two dozen of the best-known quotes from Shakespeare's plays – together with the name of the play from which they are taken:

1. 'O Romeo, Romeo! Wherefore art thou Romeo?' (*Romeo and Juliet*)

2. 'Off with his head!' (*King Richard III*)

3. 'Now is the winter of our discontent.' (*Richard III*)

4. 'This was the most unkindest cut of all.' (*Julius Caesar*)

5. 'Parting is such sweet sorrow.' (*Romeo and Juliet*)

6. 'We have seen better days.' (*Timon of Athens*)

7. 'The lady doth protest too much, methinks.' (*Hamlet*)

8. 'If music be the food of love; play on.' (*Twelfth Night*)

9. 'Once more unto the breach, dear friends, once more.' (*Henry V*)

10. 'To be or not to be, that is the question.' (*Hamlet*)

11. 'Friends, Romans, countrymen, lend me your ears.' (*Julius Caesar*)

12. 'The course of true love never did run smooth.' (*A Midsummer Night's Dream*)

13. 'Beware the Ides of March.' (*Julius Caesar*)

14. 'A horse! A horse! My kingdom for a horse!' (*Richard III*)

15. 'The first thing we do, let's kill all the lawyers.' (*Henry VI, Part 2*)

16. 'Et tu, Brute?' (*Julius Caesar*)

17. 'Lord, what fools these mortals be!' (*A Midsummer Night's Dream*)

18. 'Is this a dagger which I see before me?' (*Macbeth*)

19. 'This blessed plot, this earth, this realm, this England.' (*Richard II*)

20. 'Alas poor Yorick! I knew him, Horatio: a fellow of infinite jest, of most excellent fancy.' (*Hamlet*)

21. 'What's in a name? That which we call a rose by any other name would smell as sweet.' (*Romeo and Juliet*)

22. 'Conscience does make cowards of us all.' (*Hamlet*)

23. 'If you prick us, do we not bleed?' (*The Merchant of Venice*)

24. 'Uneasy lies the head that wears a crown.' (*Henry IV, Part 2*)

Shakespeare's Words (and their meanings).

Shakespeare used a good many unusual words. Some of the words and phrases he used he created himself. Here are some examples of Shakespeare's language:

1. A–doting – In Love.
2. Antic face – Mask.
3. Baccare! – Back! Stand back!
4. Blank – To make pale.
5. Charles' wain – The Great Bear constellation.
6. Dottard – Old fool.
7. Drumble – To dawdle.
8. Eternal jewel – Immortal soul.
9. Eyewink – Glance; notice.
10. Fancy-sick – Lovesick.
11. Felicity – Eternal bliss.
12. Gorbellied – Big-bellied.
13. Harry groat – A four-penny coin.
14. Hob and Dick – Every Tom, Dick, and Harry.
15. Hugger-mugger – Secrecy.
16. John-a-dreams – A nickname for a woolgatherer or daydreamer.
17. Jove's spreading tree – Oak tree.
18. Kidney – Type; sort.
19. Knotty-pated – Blockheaded.
20. Leaping-house – Brothel.
21. Magot-pie – Magpie.
22. Skimble-skamble – Nonsensical.
23. Slug-abed – Sleepyhead.
24. Want-wit – Idiot.

SHEPHERD'S PIE

Shepherd's pie is made with minced lamb and vegetables, with a crisp, golden topping of mashed potato. Cottage pie, which is a similar dish, is made with minced beef and not lamb. Originally, shepherd's pie was a meal that was eaten on Mondays because the meat that was used was a leftover from the Sunday joint.

SHOPS IN LONDON

A select dozen of England's most iconic shops:

1. Harrods (department store)
2. Fortnum and Masons (department store)
3. Selfridges (department store)
4. Hamleys (toy store)
5. Bates (hatters)
6. Lock and Co (hatters)
7. Foyles (book shop)
8. Hatchards (book shop)
9. Asprey (jewellers)
10. Garrards (jewellers)
11. Aquascutum (clothing store)
12. Burberry (clothing store)

SLANG

Like all languages, English has many words and phrases which are more common in speech than in writing and which are usually referred to as 'slang'. Here are a dozen examples of modern English slang:

1. Anorak – A male nerd, a committed enthusiast in a subject such as trainspotting

2. Bloater – A fat person

3. Box – Television

4. Codswallop – Nonsense

5. Buggered – Exhausted, worn out

6. As common as hen's teeth – Something rare

7. Knackered – Tired

8. Lollop – To laze around

9. Muppet – Naïve or stupid person

10. Plastered – Very drunk

11. Rag – Newspaper or magazine

12. Thick as two short planks – Stupid

SPORTS

Almost all popular sports were invented by the English. Here are just two dozen of the sports first created, played or devised by Englishmen and Englishwomen:

1. Archery

2. Badminton

3. Baseball

4. Billiards

5. Boxing

6. Cricket

7. Darts

8. Football (aka soccer)

9. Hockey

10. Horse racing

11. Motor racing

12. Mountaineering

13. Rounders

14. Rowing

15. Rugby Football

16. Sailing
17. Show jumping
18. Skiing
19. Skittles (and Ten Pin Bowling)
20. Snooker
21. Squash
22. Table tennis
23. Tennis
24. Tobogganing

The English are the only people to have been able to spread their games throughout the world. The Americans have failed to export their most important domestic sport, American football). The Australians have failed to export Australian Rules football, and the Irish have failed to find much international interest in hurling. It is generally agreed around the world that the English invented modern sport, the rules of sport and the spirit of fair play.

SPORTING HEROES

England's Dozen Greatest Sporting Heroes

1. W. G. Grace (Cricket)
2. Mike Hawthorn (Motor Racing)
3. Denis Compton (Cricket)
4. Fred Trueman (Cricket)
5. Stanley Matthews (Football)
6. J. W. H. Taylor (Golf)
7. Stirling Moss (Motor Racing)
8. William Webb Ellis (Rugby Football)
9. Tom Finney (Football)
10. Lester Piggott (Horse Racing)
11. Jim Laker (Cricket)
12. John Surtees (Motor Cycling and Motor Racing)

SPORTING TOURS

The first international sporting tour took place in 1859 when a team of English cricketers toured the United States of America.

SPOTTED DICK

The classic English pudding. There are references to a pudding resembling Spotted Dick that are 200 years old. Nobody really knows for sure why this steamed suet pudding containing raisins should be called Spotted Dick. The name 'spotted' is fairly obvious, but where did the 'Dick' come from? One explanation is that Spotted Dick used to be called Spotted Pudding, and the name 'pudding' derived from puddink or puddick. Government institutions (such as hospitals) often rename the pudding 'Spotted Richard' because they are worried about embarrassing the patients.

STARS

Many of Hollywood's most famous film stars were born in England. Here's a selection of a dozen (with their birthplace after their name):

1. Charlie Chaplin (London)
2. Cary Grant (Bristol, real name Archibald Leech)
3. Stan Laurel (Ulverston, Lancashire, real name Arthur Stanley Jefferson)
4. Charles Laughton (Scarborough, Yorkshire)
5. Bob Hope (Eltham, London)
6. Boris Karloff (London, real name William Henry Pratt)
7. Leslie Howard (London)
8. Julie Andrews (Walton on Thames, Surrey, real name Julia Elizabeth Wells)

9. Ronald Colman (Richmond, Surrey)

10. Elizabeth Taylor (London)

11. Robert Donat (Manchester, Lancashire)

12. Lawrence Olivier (Dorking, Surrey)

STARS AND STRIPES

The American national anthem was composed by John Stafford Smith, an English composer.

STATELY HOMES

England is awash with huge stately homes. In the good (or bad) old days these were occupied by large families whose needs were looked after by vast armies of servants. The richest members of the English aristocracy sometimes employed enough people to populate a decent sized village. And, indeed, they sometimes owned a decent local village so that the staff who didn't live in the house had somewhere to eat and sleep.

It has been reported that at the beginning of the 20th century the Duke of Portland employed: a steward, wine butler, under butler, groom of chambers, four footmen, two stewards' room footmen, master of the servants' hall, two pageboys, head chef, second chef, head baker, second baker, head kitchen maid, two under kitchen maids, sundry vegetable maids and scullery maids, head stillroom maid, hall porter, two hall boys, kitchen porter and six odd job men, a head housekeeper, a valet, a personal maid for the duchess and another for his daughter, a head nursery governess, French governess, a schoolroom footman, fourteen housemaids, a head window cleaner and two under window cleaners, There were 30 servants working in the stables, 30 servants in the garage, and numerous servants employed in the grounds, the laundry, the home farm and the gymnasium. The steam heating plant and electric generator in the main house required six engineers and four firemen, and the telephone exchange in the house had a telephone clerk and a telegrapher. There were also three night watchmen. Today, many of England's finest homes are open to the public while the families who own them live in a small flat hidden away somewhere in the building. It is the only way the owners can make ends meet.

Here is our list of England's dozen most magnificent homes:

1. Blenheim Palace, Woodstock, Oxfordshire
One of England's largest houses and birthplace of Sir Winston Churchill. This beautiful English Baroque-style Palace – designed by Sir John Vanbrugh and completed by Nicholas Hawksmoor – was built in the early 18th century for the 1st Duke of Marlborough, John Churchill, as a gift from Queen Anne for his victory at the Battle of Blenheim. In 1987, Blenheim Palace was designated a UNESCO World Heritage Site.

2. Castle Howard, Yorkshire
Created for the 3rd Earl of Carlisle by architect John Vanbrugh. It took 37 years to build and was completed in 1737. By the time it was completed, Vanbrugh and the 3rd Earl of Carlisle had passed away. In 1981, *Brideshead Revisited* (based on Evelyn Waugh's classic novel) was filmed here.

3. Hampton Court Palace, London
Built by Cardinal Wolsey. This beautiful palace stands on the banks of the River Thames. Hampton Court Palace has five hundred years of royal history – its most famous resident being Cardinal Wolsey's master, King Henry VIII.

4. Woburn Abbey, Bedfordshire
The ancestral home of the Dukes of Bedford. This wonderful 18th century palace was built on the foundations of a Cistercian abbey.

5. Burghley, House, Lincolnshire
Built in the 16th century. Former residence of William Cecil, spymaster of Elizabeth I. Breathtaking works of art by Antonio Verrio adorn the walls and ceilings.

6. Chatsworth, Derbyshire
Home of the Dukes of Devonshire. The first house was built here by Bess of Hardwick and her husband, Sir William Cavendish, in

the mid 16th century. Chatsworth contains one of England's finest collections of treasures, which are displayed in the many rooms throughout the house. Chatsworth is reputed to have 297 rooms, 112 fireplaces and 56 lavatories and to be lit by 2,084 lightbulbs.

7. Charlecote Park, Warwickshire
Home to the Lucy family for over 700 years. Charlecote Park is set alongside the River Avon. Its beautiful grounds were landscaped by 'Capability Brown'.

8. Blickling Hall, Norfolk
This red brick Jacobean mansion stands on the site where Anne Boylen's childhood home used to be. Blickling Hall was built in 1616-28 and was designed by Robert Lyminge.

9. Cottesbrooke Hall, Northamptonshire
Believed to have been the model for Jane Austin's, *Mansfield Park*. The building of this magnificent Queen Anne house was begun in 1702 and completed in 1713.

10. Hatfield House, Hertfordshire
Built at the beginning of the 17th century by Robert Cecil the First Earl of Salisbury, it has been home to the Cecil family ever since. Part of the Royal Palace of Hatfield, which is not far from Hatfield House, still exists and was the childhood home of Queen Elizabeth I.

11. Longleat House, Wiltshire
Home of the Marquess of Bath. Longleat is famed for its wonderful house and safari park. Longleat House was built in the late 16th century by Sir John Thynne.

12. Althorp, Northamptonshire
Home of the Spencer family for nearly 500 years. Lady Diana Spencer is laid to rest at Althorp on an island in the middle of the lake in the grounds.

STONEHENGE

Half a Dozen Facts

1. Stonehenge, England's greatest prehistoric monumental mystery, dominates Salisbury Plain in the county of Wiltshire, England. It is believed that Stonehenge was built around 4,500 years ago.

2. Archaeologists agree that Stonehenge was built in three phases with the first phase comprising a circular ditch, a bank and 56 pits known as Aubrey Holes. In the 1920's, excavations of Stonehenge uncovered cremated human bones buried inside the 56 Aubrey Holes. Since then, around 240 human remains have been found at Stonehenge. Recent research has discovered that they were buried over a period of five centuries, giving credence to the theory that Stonehenge was a burial ground for the elite of the population.

3. An aerial view of the main 'building' of Stonehenge, taken before it became a ruin, would have clearly shown an outer circle of Sarsen stones (believed to have come from the Marlborough Downs near Avebury in Wiltshire) with lintels resting continuously along the tops of the stones. Just inside the Sarsen circle was a circle – without lintels – of bluestones which are much smaller than the Sarsen stones. (The bluestones were so named because of their distinct colour). Inside the bluestone circle were trilithons of Sarsen stones, which were arranged symmetrically in a horseshoe shape (a trilithon comprising two erect stones underneath a horizontal lintel). Immediately within the Sarsen horseshoe was a horseshoe of erect bluestones without lintels. And lastly, came the 16ft high 'Altar' stone. Today, the once upright Altar stone lies in the surface of the ground, broken in two. Sadly, over the centuries, many of the original stones at Stonehenge have fallen over or have gone missing.

4. Recent research suggests that it was about 2300 BC that saw the arrival of the first stone circle – the bluestones from Preseli in South Wales. The transportation of the stones to Stonehenge was incredible, considering that the largest Sarsen stone weighs as much as 50 tons. How they did it, one can only speculate. During the different phases of the construction of Stonehenge,

there were no cranes, hoists or machinery. It was an amazing feat of building work that would have required vast amounts of manual labour. It is thought that the building of Stonehenge was finally completed around 1600 BC.

5. There have been many theories as to why Stonehenge was built but none of these theories has ever been proven. Some of the suggestions are that Stonehenge was a temple, a place of healing, a domain for the spirits of the dead, and an astronomical observatory.

6. In 1915, local landowner, Cecil Chubb, bought Stonehenge for £6,600 after the previous owner Sir Edmund Antrobus died. Three years later, Cecil Chubb gave Stonehenge to the nation. One of the conditions was that the entrance fee should be no more than a shilling.

SUNDAY ROAST DINNER

The Sunday roast is believed to have originated in Yorkshire. Usually eaten during the middle of the day or early afternoon the meal comprises meat, roast potatoes, Yorkshire pudding, two different types of vegetable and gravy. The most popular meat for the Sunday roast is beef.

TAXIS

A dozen facts about the London black cab:

1. The hackney coach was the first 'black taxi' in London in the 17th century. Captain Bailey was the creator of the first taxi rank by bringing four of his hackney coaches out of the tavern yards and into the open in the Strand, outside Maypole Inn.

2. It was Oliver Cromwell who made taxi driving a profession by setting up the Fellowship of Master Hackney Coachmen by Act of Parliament. Three years later, a second Act was brought in under Charles II which required coaches to be licensed. The

London black taxi trade is the oldest regulated public transport system in the world.

3. The word 'cab' is an abbreviation of the French word 'cabriolet'. Cabriolets, light two-wheeled carriages with hoods and drawn by one horse, replaced the hackney coaches at the beginning of the 19th century. The word taxi comes from the taximeter which Wilhelm Bruhn invented in the late 19th century as a way of measuring people's cab fares.

4. Before qualifying for a London black cab licence a driver must be of good character, have a clean driver's licence and have no criminal record. To qualify for a licence, a would-be cabbie must pass probably the most difficult driving test in existence. In addition, prospective cab drivers must acquire the Knowledge of London (known simply as The Knowledge). The Knowledge, which was introduced in 1851, requires drivers to learn the details of 25,000 streets as well as hotels, clubs, restaurants, theatres, parks, hospitals, colleges, places of worship, government buildings, etc., within a six mile radius of Charing Cross Station. On average, it takes about three years to complete The Knowledge. Once qualified, it is considered bad luck if the taxi driver doesn't do his or her first job without charge.

5. Traditional London black cabs (licensed by the Public Carriage Office) are the only taxis allowed to ply for hire in London. Cab drivers have to wear their seatbelts travelling from and to work, but they don't have to wear their seatbelts whilst working.

6. Although advertising is allowed on the sides of the cab, advertising is not allowed on the boot, in case it obscures the registration number or the licence plate.

7. All London black cabs have to have a passenger compartment high enough to enable a customer wearing a bowler hat to sit comfortably inside. All London black cabs have to be wheelchair accessible.

8. In 1976, the law requiring a cab driver to carry a bale of hay on the roof of his cab to feed the horse was repealed. Cab drivers are also no longer required to carry a sack of oats or a nosebag on the side of their vehicle. The law was brought in during

the time when black cabs used to be carriages pulled by horses (hackney coaches).

9. Even if the 'for hire' indicator light is on, the cab driver is not legally obliged to stop after being hailed. A cab is not technically 'plying for trade' while it is moving.

10. The black cab has a 25ft turning circle which means that it can do a U-turn off a central rank.

11. By law, a cabbie is required to search his cab for lost property after each hiring.

12. Once a year, every taxi in London is thoroughly checked before being issued with a new licence. The test is much stricter than the MOT test for private vehicles.

TAXI DRIVERS

London taxi drivers (black cab drivers) have a language of their own. Here are some examples of their 'lingo':

- To Bilk – To avoid paying the fare.
- Bowler hat – A businessman.
- Broom off – To refuse to take a passenger.
- Butter boy – A new, inexperienced cabbie.
- Flyer – A fare to Gatwick or Heathrow airport.
- Gasworks – Houses of Parliament.
- Kipper season – A period when trade is quiet. The worst months of the year for cab drivers are usually January, February and March.
- Legal – Pay the correct fare without giving a tip.
- Musher – A driver who owns their cab.
- Pancake – St Pancras Station.
- Single pin – One person.
- Wedding Cake – The Victoria Memorial in front of Buckingham Palace.

TEA

Tea is England's national drink. At times of crisis the English will always sit down and have a 'nice cup of tea'. Here are a dozen facts about our favourite English brew:

1. Tea originated in China, and was established as the national drink of China under the Tang Dynasty (618-906AD). According to Chinese legend, it was the Chinese Emperor, Shen Nung, who first discovered tea around 2737 BC. Some leaves had blown from a nearby Camellia sinensis bush into the pot of boiled drinking water that the Emperor's servant had prepared for his master. Shen Nung stopped his servant from throwing the water away because, being a keen herbalist, he was curious to know what the infusion tasted like. To his surprise, the Emperor thought the brew wonderfully refreshing. And, so, tea was born.

2. In 1664, the East India Company first commenced importing tea into England.

3. In 1657, Thomas Garaway, of Garaway's Coffee House in London was the first person to sell tea in England.

4. In 1689, the Government imposed a tax on tea bought and drunk in England. As a result, tea became so expensive that it was only popular among the upper classes. At one point, tax on tea was so high that sales almost stopped completely. By the 18th century, however, tea drinking had become very popular in England, though the high taxes meant that many people found it difficult to afford. This resulted in tea smuggling and tea adulteration by criminal gangs. Sheep dung was even used in tea adulteration. It was Prime Minister, William Pitt the Younger who stopped tea smuggling overnight by dramatically slashing the huge rate of tax on tea.

5. There are many flavours and varieties of tea. Earl Grey tea is a blend of China tea with a distinctive aroma and flavour which comes from the addition of oil extracted from the rind of the bergamot orange. Earl Grey tea is named after the 2nd Earl Grey, British Prime Minister in the 1830s, who received a gift of the flavoured tea in the early 19th century.

6. China is the largest producer of tea in the world: producing around 1,160,000 tons a year.

7. By the 18th century, tea had become the most popular beverage (beating gin and ale) in England.

8. Only 30% of tea drinkers take sugar in their tea.

9. In 1908, tea merchant, Thomas Sullivan, invented the teabag by accident. In order to cut costs, he put samples of dried tea leaves in silken bags to give to potential customers. Some of his customers placed the silken bags into cups of hot water not realising that they had to remove the tea from the bags first. The only complaint Thomas Sullivan received was that he should have used a coarser weave to help aid the brewing process.

10. Tea contains half the caffeine of brewed coffee.

11. Ever since tea became popular in England, tea-drinkers have argued about whether to add milk before or after the tea is in the cup. Today, the experts say that if a tea bag is being used the milk should be added after the bag has brewed. If the milk is added too early it will lower the temperature and affect the brewing process.

12. Some people are confused as to whether they should just raise the teacup when taking a sip, or raise the teacup and the saucer. English tea drinking protocol dictates that when seated at a table one should only raise the teacup when sipping tea. The teacup should be placed back onto the saucer in between sips. Never, ever wave your cup in the air, leave your teaspoon in your cup, slurp your tea or – the crudest of all – drink tea from your saucer.

TELEGRAPH

The electric telegraph was invented by an Englishman called Charles Wheatstone. Charles Wheatstone (1802-1875) was born in Gloucester, and in 1829 he suggested building a telegraph between London and Edinburgh to enable people in the south of England to talk to people in Scotland. He called the arrangement a 'telephone'.

(Alexander Graham Bell is officially regarded as having invented the telephone in 1876 but it was Wheatstone who had the idea for it and thought up the name.)

Wheatstone began the experiments that would lead to the electric telegraph in 1835, suggesting that the device would be extremely useful for transmitting information around the world. To test the invention an experimental line was set up between two railway stations; one in Camden Town and one at Euston, and on 25th July 1837 the first trial took place. Wheatstone, sitting at Euston, sent the first message and his business partner, Cooke, in Camden, replied.

Gradually, railway companies realised the potential value of the telegraph and started to install lines between their stations. The invention soon became an invaluable part of public life. In 1840, Wheatstone suggested laying a line from Dover to Calais and in 1859 Wheatstone was asked by the Government to report on the idea of a cable across the Atlantic.

Seven years later, an American called Samuel Morse demonstrated a similar system, along a railway track, just as Wheatstone and Clarke had done. Despite the fact that he was obviously not the real inventor, Morse fought vigorously but dishonestly to be described as the inventor of the telegraph.

THE RED TELEPHONE BOX
Half a Dozen Facts

1. The familiar red telephone box was designed by Sir Giles Gilbert Scott in the 1920's in response to a competition organised by the Post Office.

2. Sir Giles Gilbert Scott was the architect who also designed Liverpool's Gothic Anglican Cathedral, Waterloo Bridge and Battersea Power Station. Sir Giles Gilbert Scott's grandfather, Sir George Scott, was the architect who designed the Albert Memorial in London.

3. It was the Post Office which insisted that the telephone boxes should be red. Sir Giles Gilbert Scott had suggested silver.

4. The iconic red box has a domed roof and the name 'telephone'

on each of the four sides. Just above the word 'telephone' is an image of the royal crown.

5. British Telecom replaced most of the red boxes during the latter part of the 20th century, explaining that they wanted public telephone boxes that were more difficult to vandalise and easier to maintain.

6. The classic red telephone box can be found in many places around the world – including Malta, Bermuda and Gibraltar. There is a red telephone box outside the British Embassy in Washington, America.

THRILLER AND CRIME WRITERS

England has produced more than its fair share of the world's greatest thriller and crime writers. Here are our favourites (with real names alongside where appropriate):

- Eric Ambler
- John le Carré (David Cornwell)
- Len Deighton
- Clive Egleton
- Agatha Christie
- Dornford Yates (Cecil Mercer)
- Sapper (Herman Cyril McNeile)
- Adam Hall (Trevor Dudley-Smith)
- William Haggard (Richard Clayton)
- Geoffrey Household
- William le Queux
- James Hadley Chase (Rene Raymond)

TOAD-IN-THE-HOLE

Toad-in-the-hole is a dish consisting of small sausages cooked in a crisp, golden brown Yorkshire pudding batter, usually served with vegetables and gravy. Nobody really knows for sure the origin of the dish's comical name. However, it is widely believed that the name is due to the appearance of the dish, i.e. the sausages in batter resembling toads sticking their heads out of holes. It is thought that the practise of putting meat in batter or pastry dates back to Roman times.

THE TOWER OF LONDON
A Dozen Facts

1. The Tower of London, home to the Crown Jewels (since 1303), is situated outside the old London city wall on the northern bank of the River Thames.

2. William the Conqueror ordered the construction of the inner keep, the 'White Tower', in 1078 in order to control and protect London. More buildings were added later by successive monarchs.

3. The White Tower is one of 21 towers of the building complex, and is the largest and most significant tower. The White Tower is approximately 90ft high. The White Tower acquired its name from the original building material of white stone from Normandy.

4. Throughout its life the Tower of London has fulfilled many roles, including: a fortress (its primary use), a royal palace, a prison, a treasury, a royal mint and a zoo. Although no longer inhabited by the royals, the Tower of London is still officially a royal residence.

5. Some of the well-known people who have been executed at the Tower of London include: Henry VI, Sir Thomas More, Anne Boleyn, Catherine Howard, Lord Lovat and Lady Jane Grey. Executions were carried out within the Tower's grounds on Tower Green and outside behind the Castle on Tower Hill.

Only the privileged (if you can call it that) were executed within the Tower's grounds.

6. The last execution at the Tower of London took place in 1941. The execution was that of a German spy called Josef Jakobs.

7. The tragic princes, Edward V and his younger brother, who were 10 and 12 at the time, were believed to have been murdered at the Tower of London. Their skeletons were discovered about three centuries ago.

8. Sir Walter Ralegh was imprisoned twice at the Tower of London. During his second incarceration he wrote *The History of the World*.

9. The Kray twins were imprisoned briefly in the Tower of London in 1952 for failing to report for national service.

10. Ravens reside at the Tower and have done for centuries. Legend has it that there should always be at least six ravens at the Tower of London and if they should disappear, then the Tower will crumble and the Kingdom of England will fall. The ravens at the Tower have their wings clipped to prevent them from escaping and to keep England intact. The ravens are very well looked after by the Tower of London's Yeoman Warder Ravenmaster.

11. The Tower of London is believed to be the most haunted building in England. Queen Anne Boleyn has reputedly been seen wondering around with her head under her arm. Some of the other ghosts include: Lady Jane Grey, the Princes in the Tower and Henry VI. A phantom bear has even been seen.

12. The Yeoman Warders (often referred to as beefeaters) guard the Tower of London. Every evening, they are responsible for closing the main gate. The closing of the main gate is called the Ceremony of the Keys. This ritual has taken place for 700 years.

TROLLOPE, ANTHONY (1815-1892)

Anthony Trollope was a peculiarly English author who invented the idea of a series of novels following the adventures and lives of the same characters. His most successful novels include the *Barchester* series (*Barchester Towers*, *Doctor Thorne*, *Framley Parsonage*, *The Small House at Allington* and the *Last Chronicle of Barset*) which are all set in the West Country, and the *Palliser* novels which are named after the main hero, Plantaganet Palliser. Although he was enormously successful as an author, Trollope had a day job: he worked for the Post Office where, among other things, he invented the pillar-box. In addition to his daily work administering the mail, he wrote for three hours every day. He even had a special desk made to clip onto his saddle so that he could write as he wandered around the countryside inspecting rural post offices.

TWO FINGERS

The best known hand gesture in the world – a V sign formed with the aid of the middle finger and forefinger – was first used by English archers at the battle of Agincourt in 1415. The English waved the fingers to show they still had their two bow fingers and could, therefore, still fire arrows. If the English archers had been captured, the French would have cut off these two fingers to prevent them using a bow and arrow again.

UMBRELLA

A tightly-furled black umbrella is synonymous with the idea of the English gentleman. It is a tradition that goes back nearly 300 years.

First invented over four thousand years ago, early umbrellas were designed to provide shade from the sun ('Umbra' means shade or shadow in Latin) but the English climate meant that pedestrians needed protection from the rain rather than the sun.

The first English umbrella, often known as a Hanway (after Jonas Hanway), had an oiled canvas and a frame that was made of whalebone and wood. As you can imagine, it was very heavy to carry. Hanway, who was born in Portsmouth in 1712, was a philanthropist who founded the Marine Society. He was the first man in England who was brave enough to carry an umbrella on a daily basis. Up until that time, umbrellas were considered to be feminine accessories.

Hanway had to put up with many jibes from the public before umbrella carrying became commonplace. Coachmen were especially scornful because they were worried that the umbrella would become popular and, thus, affect their trade. However, thanks to Jonas Hanway, the umbrella eventually came to be regarded as a 'good idea' and later became synonymous with the English gentleman.

In 1852, Samuel Fox invented the steel frame for the umbrella.

Colloquial names used in England for umbrellas include: 'gamp' (after Mrs Gamp, the Charles Dickens character in *Martin Chuzzlewit* who often carries an umbrella) and 'brolly' (which is the most common term used). The Cockney rhyming slang for umbrella is 'Auntie Ella'.

In Victorian times umbrellas, like walking sticks, were sometimes fitted with added extras such as drinking flasks, swords and compasses and were often decorated with silver or bone handles.

LONDON UNDERGROUND

Around 150,000 items are lost every year on the London Underground. Here are a dozen of some of the oddest items which have been found abandoned by travellers:

1. Park bench
2. Stuffed eagle
3. Pair of breast implants
4. A 14ft boat
5. Grandfather clock
6. Vasectomy kit
7. Lawnmower
8. Inflatable doll (fully inflated)

9. Chinese typewriter

10. Divan bed

11. Bishop's crook

12. Coffin (empty)

UXBRIDGE, LORD

Few things sum up 'Englishness' better than this exchange between Lord Uxbridge and the Duke of Wellington, at the battle of Waterloo.

Lord Uxbridge: *'By God, Sir. I've lost my leg.'*

Duke of Wellington: *'By God, Sir. So you have.'*

VICTORIA (1819-1901)

Queen Victoria's reign saw the birth of the modern world. She grew up to reign over the largest empire in the history of the world. She wanted England to be dominant and she believed it was the nation's destiny to rule as much of the world as possible. Victoria's empire was an empire based on trade; the English had acquired naval bases, colonies and coaling stations around the globe. The Queen's ambitions for England were realised. Well before her death, the English had become the richest and most powerful people in the world. In 1897, at Queen Victoria's Diamond Jubilee, the fleet formed five lines, each five miles long, and it took them four hours to pass in review at Spithead. England was the centre of the world. Money was brought to London to be banked. London insured everything. Cartographers coloured England's territories pink on the maps. England ruled a quarter of the earth's total land area and included a quarter of the world's population. The Empire, created largely under Queen Victoria, was far bigger than anything ever put together by the Russians, the Spanish, the French, the Americans, the Japanese, the Portuguese or, indeed, any other country. Here are a dozen facts about Queen Victoria:

1. Queen Victoria – Queen of Great Britain and Ireland, and later, with the help of Tory Minister, Benjamin Disraeli, Empress of India – was born on 24 May 1819 at Kensington Palace.

2. Queen Victoria's father was Edward Augustus, Duke of Kent (King George III's son). Her mother was the widowed Princess Victoria of Saxe-Coburg-Saalfeld. Queen Victoria was Christened Alexandrina Victoria (nicknamed Drina throughout her childhood) and was her father's only legitimate child.

3. Queen Victoria was fifth in line to the throne when she was born.

4. The young Victoria had a lonely childhood, without many children of her own age to play with; her half siblings were quite a lot older than her. Instead, the young princess had a vast collection of dolls for company.

5. Right up until her succession to the throne, Queen Victoria slept every night in the same room as her mother. She was not allowed to walk downstairs or upstairs without somebody holding her hand. Her mother wanted to protect her daughter from any physical harm. She firmly believed her daughter would one day be Queen.

6. The tiny (she was just 4ft 11in tall) Princess acceded to the throne in 1837 after her uncle, King William IV, died. Queen Victoria wrote about the news of her accession in her journal (which she religiously kept throughout her life): 'Since it has pleased providence to place me in this station, I shall do my utmost to fulfil my duty towards my country; I am very young and perhaps in many, though not all things, inexperienced, but I am sure that very few have more real good will and more real desire to do what is fit and right than I have.'

7. It was Queen Victoria who proposed to her first cousin Prince Albert of Saxe-Coburg and Gotha. She had to do this because royal etiquette would not allow the Prince to propose to the Queen. On seeing Prince Albert during his visit on October 10th 1839, she later wrote in her journal: 'It was with some emotion that I beheld Albert – who is beautiful'.

8. Queen Victoria and Prince Albert were married on February

10th 1840 in the Chapel Royal at St James's Palace. Queen Victoria grew to depend a great deal on Prince Albert for advice and guidance. Royal policy was his policy and Albert had a great deal of influence. It was Prince Albert who helped to popularise the Christmas tree throughout England.

9. Queen Victoria and Prince Albert went on to have nine children: five girls and four boys. Queen Victoria used chloroform when giving birth to her eighth child, Prince Leopold, in 1853. The chloroform was administered by English physician, Dr John Snow. Despite public outcry from religious moralists who believed that women should endure pain when giving birth, Victoria used chloroform again when giving birth to her ninth and final child.

10. Queen Victoria survived seven assassination attempts. The first assassination attempt was by 18-year-old Edward Oxford. He fired a shot at Queen Victoria and Prince Albert from one of the two pistols he was carrying. He was sentenced to 27 years in a mental asylum for his crime.

11. Sadly, Prince Albert (who had become the Prince Consort when Victoria became Queen) died from typhoid fever on December 14th 1861 at the age of 42. Queen Victoria did not attend her husband's funeral because it was established protocol for women not to attend funerals in the 19th century. In mourning for her beloved husband, Queen Victoria withdrew from the political and social scene for quite some time, and wore black for the remaining 40 years of her life (even wearing black to her children's weddings).

12. Queen Victoria reigned as British monarch for 63 years. She was 81 when she died from a stroke on January 22nd 1901 at Osborne House in the Isle of Wight. The Queen was buried with an alabaster of Prince Albert's hand (that was placed into her hand) and with some personal mementoes, which she had requested be buried with her.

VICTORIAN GIFTS

The English Victorians gave to the world:

1. The post office
2. The police
3. Clean drinking water
4. Sewers
5. Railways and railway stations
6. Metalled roads
7. Agricultural machinery
8. Street lighting
9. Electricity
10. Antisepsis in hospitals
11. Iron ships
12. The telegraph

VICTORIA'S LANDS

No one has more square miles of the planet earth named after him or her than Queen Victoria. The total area named after her is approximately 1,250,000 square miles. The half dozen biggest areas are:

1. Queensland (Australia)
2. Victoria (Australia)
3. Great Victoria Desert (Australia)
4. Victoria Island (Canada)
5. Lake Victoria and Victoria Falls (Africa)
6. Victoria Strait (Canada)

VILLAGES

England's Dozen Most Magnificent Villages

1. Polperro, Cornwall
An exquisite 13th century fishing village which attracts tens of thousands of holidaymakers every year. Polperro, with its beautiful harbour, has a Saxon bridge across the river Poll, a 'House on Props', and a former fisherman's home that is covered in a great many shells.

2. Castle Combe, Wiltshire
Its enchanting display of stone-built cottages make visitors feel that they have slipped back in time. In 2001, Castle Combe – made famous by the film Dr Doolittle – was voted 'Most Picturesque Village' in the country.

3. Clovelly, Devon
This beautiful fishing village is mainly esteemed for its wonderfully majestic, steep, cobbled main-street. Clovelly was the former home of the author Charles Kingsley who wrote such novels as *The Water Babies* and *Westward Ho!* Charles Dickens was a fan of Clovelly.

4. Amberley, Sussex
This pretty, peaceful, picturesque village, once a major centre for lime production, has been called the 'Pearl of Sussex'. The surrounding landscape of Amberley village is dominated by a 600-year-old castle, which is now run as a hotel.

5. Dunster, Somerset
A majestic, medieval village well-known for its Yarn Market which stands in the middle of High Street. The Yarn Market has been standing there since 1580.

6. Finchingfield, Essex
An enigmatic former spinning village where no two buildings are exactly alike. A beautiful white windmill, dating from 1756, is the village's main attraction.

7. Godshill, Isle of Wight

Attractive thatched greystone cottages stand nearby the largest church on the Isle of Wight, which is the 14th century Church of All Saints. The church is home to a spectacular 500-year-old wall painting of Christ on the Cross.

8. Ashby St Ledgers, Northamptonshire

An array of beautiful, amber-coloured ironstone-built cottages adorn this pretty village. However, pretty as the cottages are, the village's main attraction are the fascinating paintings that decorate the Norman tower walls of the Church of the Blessed Virgin Mary and St Leodegarius.

9. Honington, Warwickshire

Has often won the title of Warwickshire's Best Kept Village. Honington, a former estate village serving the successive proprietors of Honington Hall, is exceptionally pretty and tranquil. A true delight.

10. Eardisland, Herefordshire

Often voted the prettiest village in the Midlands. Sixteenth century timber and plaster cottages sit alongside the tranquil river Arrow.

11. Snowshill, Gloucestershire

The 19th century Church of St Barnabus is surrounded by beautiful cottages built of limestone. This magnificent village has appeared in several film and television productions.

12. Thornton Le Dale, Yorkshire

Widely regarded as one of the prettiest villages in the North Riding.

WASSAIL

For centuries the wassail bowl was carried from door to door on New Year's Day in England. The sharing of the contents of the bowl was accompanied by much singing and merriment (not surprising when you see the contents). Carrying a bowl of potent brew from door to door may now contravene a good many health and safety regulations, but there is no reason why you can't carry on wassailing at home. So, here's a very old traditional recipe for wassail as it has been served in England for several centuries.

1. Put into a cauldron a quart of old ale. (There is something reassuring about any recipe which starts with the words 'put into a cauldron'. If you don't have a cauldron handy you can, if you wish substitute a large pan.)

2. Add a bag of spices containing a piece of orange peel, a piece of lemon peel, 6 cloves, 6 pepper corns, a whole ginger (the size of a hazelnut), a slip of cinnamon and a piece of nutmeg.

3. Add a full desert spoon of honey.

4. Bring to the boil.

5. While the mixture in the pan is warming up, put the yolks of three eggs in a large bowl.

6. When the mixture is just about to boil pour it over the eggs, stirring with a wooden spoon as you do so.

7. When the mixture is thickened add half a pint of spirits (you can choose from rum, whisky, gin and brandy).

8. Ladle out nice and warm (but not so hot that you burn yourself.)

9. If not sweet enough, add more honey.

10. Sing and make merry.

WESTMINSTER BRIDGE
Half a Dozen Facts

1. Westminster Bridge, which crosses the River Thames in London, is 827ft long and 84ft wide.

2. The present bridge dates from 1862 and replaced Charles Labelye's beautiful stone bridge, which was considered to be unsafe. Work started on the 'new' Westminster Bridge in 1854.

3. The present Westminster Bridge was designed by Thomas Page.

4. Westminster Bridge is now the oldest bridge in use in London.

5. The seven-arch wrought iron bridge has gothic detailing by the architect of the Palace of Westminster, Charles Barry.

6. The bridge is painted green in homage to the colour of the benches in the Houses of Commons.

WESTMINSTER PALACE
A Dozen Facts

1. The Palace of Westminster is a large complex of buildings in London that is home to the House of Commons and the House of Lords.

2. The Palace stands on the site where Edward the Confessor had a palace built in the 11th century.

3. The Palace of Westminster is situated on the north bank of the River Thames in the London borough of the City of Westminster.

4. The south end of the Palace of Westminster has the 336ft high Victoria Tower and the north side has the iconic Big Ben.

5. Whenever Parliament is in session, a Union Jack flies from the Victoria Tower by day and the Ayrton light on the top of Big Ben shines by night.

6. The neo-Gothic style Palace of Westminster (commonly known as the Houses of Parliament) was the main royal residence from the time of Edward the Confessor to the early reign of Henry VIII. It was then adopted as the assembly place for the House of Lords and the House of Commons.

7. The House of Commons used to assemble in the Royal Chapel of St Stephen within Westminster until a fire broke out in 1834 and destroyed the Palace of Westminster. Only Westminster Hall, the Jewel Tower, the crypt of St Stephen's Chapel and the adjacent cloisters survived.

8. The 'New Palace' was built over the next 30 years. Architect Charles Barry and interior designer Augustus Welby Pugin were responsible for the Palace.

9. Westminster Hall is almost the only part of the ancient Palace of Westminster which survives in its original state. It is here that eminent statesmen and monarchs lie in state. For example, Winston Churchill lay in state at Westminster Hall after his death in 1965.

10. The 240ft by 67ft Westminster Hall has witnessed some of the most dramatic incidents in English history. It was there, for example, that King Charles I heard himself condemned to execution. The Hall has managed to survive a fire, death-watch beetles and, during the Second World War, bomb attacks.

11. The Palace of Westminster contains over 1,100 rooms and 100 staircases. The Palace even has a hair salon and a gymnasium. It is also home to a number of bars and restaurants.

12. The expression 'to toe the line' originated in the House of Commons. On the floor of the House of Commons are two red lines, which are just over two sword lengths apart. Decorum dictates that MPs are not allowed to cross these lines when speaking. This rule was originally enforced to prevent duels from occurring. If an MP steps across the line while giving a speech, he or she will be shouted down by members of the opposition.

WESTWARD HO!

Westward Ho! is the name of a seaside village near Bideford in North Devon. It is unique for two reasons. First, it is the only town in England which has an exclamation mark as part of its name. Second, the town was named after a book (rather than the other way round). Charles Kingsley's historical novel *Westward Ho!* was published in 1855. The title wasn't original when Kingsley used it. Two and a half centuries earlier George Chapman, Ben Jonson and John Marston had written a play called *Eastward Ho!* which was, in turn, a satirical response to an even earlier play called *Westward Ho!* and written by John Webster and Thomas Dekker. Charles Kingsley was born in Devon and is also the author of *The Water Babies* which was published in 1863.

WODEHOUSE P. G. (1881-1975)
A Dozen Facts

1. P. G. Wodehouse gave the world Bertie Wooster, Jeeves the valet, Lord Emsworth, Aunt Agatha, Ukridge, Mr Mulliner and Psmith. Wodehouse is almost certainly the only author in the history of literature to have created a legendary character (the Empress of Blandings) who happens to be a pig.

2. Pelham Grenville Wodehouse (also known as Plum) wrote over one hundred books (including eleven novels and 35 short stories about his most famous creations, Jeeves and Bertie Wooster).

3. Wodehouse also worked as a lyricist and librettist with Cole Porter, Ivor Novello, Irving Berlin and Jerome Kern on many successful Broadway shows. Wodehouse was regarded by Ira Gershwin, Oscar Hammerstein II, Cole Porter and Richard Rogers as their mentor and a most significant figure in the development of the American musical.

4. The name Wodehouse is pronounced Woodhouse. The soubriquet 'Plum' (by which Wodehouse was widely known) comes from the way the young Wodehouse tried, without great success, to pronounce his first Christian name.

5. During World War II, Wodehouse and his wife stayed at their home in Le Touquet as the Germans swept through northern France. Their pet parrot attacked a German officer and the Wodehouses were arrested and taken to Berlin. Wodehouse was allowed to make a series of five rather bright and breezy broadcasts about life in captivity. They were intended to be comforting and encouraging to his English speaking audience. In England, people in high places took exception to his broadcasting

from Berlin, mistakenly and rather stupidly assuming that this meant that he was a Nazi supporter.

6. The world which Wodehouse created is unique. It seems real enough, and some of the characters are doubtless based, in some way, on people Wodehouse had met. But although everything in it is consistent and convincing, it is a parallel universe, positioned at another angle to reality. In Wodehouse country it is always spring, the weather is always sunny and houses and clubs are full of young men in spats. Characters in Wodehouse books include: Catsmeat Potter-Pirbright, Dogface Rainsby, Bingo Little, Oofy Prosser, Gussie Fink-Nottle, Pongo Twistleton-Twistleton and Barmy Fotheringay-Phipps. They lived in an England that never existed, and never could, in a season of everlasting merriment.

7. Jeeves, the butler who shimmers, floats, filters or oozes into rooms, rather than merely entering in the way that mortals do, understands all. He knows everything (his bedtime reading includes Spinoza and Nietzsche) and can make a pick-me-up capable of eradicating the worst of hangovers. Bertie Wooster is defined by two basic principles: never let down a chum (or even an aunt), and never scorn a woman's love, however misguided, misplaced or unwelcome it might be. It is these basic, tightly-held, principles which lead Bertie into so many scrapes.

8. It is Wodehouse's writing style which makes his books what they are. Generations of authors have regarded him as their idol. Evelyn Waugh described him, simply, as 'the Master'. His plots are far more complex than they seem and Wodehouse created memorable characters in a way that no one before or since has managed. The girls are either sweetly dottie (describing the stars in the sky as 'God's little daisy chain') or as tough as old boots, but not as good looking. Aunts are always overbearing and demanding (as in Aunt Agatha) though sometimes possessing a slightly softer side (as in Aunt Dahlia).

9. Open any Wodehouse book at any page you will instantly find a stream of brilliant and original word pictures leaping at you from the page. 'Uncle Tom always looked like a pterodactyl with a secret sorrow'. An unsuitably coloured tie is described by Jeeves

as 'rather sudden'. The writing, carefully crafted, meticulously reworked by a genius with a craftsman's patience, always appears utterly effortless.

10. Wodehouse was a gentle man and a lover of all animals, particularly cats and dogs. He was also a mad-keen cricketer (he was a good club batsman and medium pace bowler and co-founder of the Hollywood Cricket Club). He genuinely seemed to live in an imaginary world of his own. Like many writers he lived (and loved) a rather boring, stable, ritualistic life, spreading his wings in his plots and the imaginary world he had created. Early in his life he bought a Darracq motorcar with his earnings. He paid £450 for it (a huge sum at the time) and drove it into a hedge after taking a single lesson. He never drove it again and, for the rest of his life, preferred to be driven.

11. P. G. Wodehouse, one of the world's most successful authors, belatedly received his much deserved knighthood just before he died, at the age of 93.

12. Today, reference to his work, and his characters, appear daily throughout the world. For example, the *Oxford English Dictionary* contains more than 1,600 Wodehouse quotations.

Two Dozen Quotes from P. G. Wodehouse

No author is more English than P. G. Wodehouse. No author better exemplifies English humour. Here are two dozen quotes showing just why professional authors regard P. G. Wodehouse as the indisputable master of their trade:

1. 'Go and get your hair cut,' screamed Beatrice. 'You look like a chrysanthemum.' *Hot Water*

2. 'You're too clever for one man. You ought to incorporate.' *The Small Bachelor*

3. 'Honoria Glossop is one of those robust, dynamic girls with the muscles of a welter-weight and a laugh like a squadron of cavalry charging over a tin bridge.' *Carry On, Jeeves*

4. 'Warm though the morning was, he shivered, as only a confirmed bachelor gazing into the naked face of matrimony can shiver.' *The Old Reliable*

5. 'He tottered blindly towards the bar like a camel making for an oasis after a hard day at the office.' *Plum Pie*

6. 'He gave me the sort of look a batsman gives an umpire when he gives him out leg-before-wicket.' *Concealed Art*

7. 'What a curse these social distinctions are. They ought to be abolished. I remember saying that to Karl Marx once, and he thought there might be a book in it.' *Quick Service*

8. 'Unlike the male codfish, which, suddenly finding itself the parent of three million five hundred thousand little codfish, cheerfully resolves to love them all, the British aristocracy is apt to look with a somewhat jaundiced eye on its younger sons.' *Blandings Castle and Elsewhere*

9. 'Golf...is the infallible test. The man who can go into a path of rough alone, with the knowledge that only God is watching him, and play his ball where it lies, is the man who will serve you faithfully and well.' *The Clicking of Cuthbert*

10. 'Beach the butler was a man who had made two chins grow where only one had been before, and his waistcoat swelled like the sail of a racing yacht.' *Galahad at Blandings*

11. 'A woman's smile is like a bath-tap. Turn it on and you find yourself in hot water.' *Candlelight*

12. 'As Egbert from boyhood up had shown no signs of possessing any intelligence whatsoever, a place had been found for him in the Civil Service.' *The World of Mr Mulliner*

13. 'I can't do with any more education. I was full up years ago.' *The Code of the Woosters*

14. 'Why do you want a political career? Have you ever been in the House of Commons and taken a good look at the inmates? As weird a gaggle of freaks and sub-humans as was ever collected in one spot.' *Cocktail Time*

15. 'He resembled a minor prophet who has been hit behind the ear by a stuffed eelskin.' *Ukridge*

16. 'The first rule in buying Christmas presents is to select something shiny. If the chosen object is of leather, the leather must look as if it had been well greased; if it is of silver it must gleam with the light that never was on land or sea. This is because the wariest person will often mistake shininess for expensiveness.' *Louder and Funnier*

17. 'Love is like life assurance. The older you are when you start it, the more it costs.' *Don't Listen, Ladies*

18. 'Into the face of the young man who sat on the terrace at the Hotel Magnifique at Cannes there had crept a look of furtive shame, the shifty, hangdog look which announces that an Englishman is about to talk French.' *The Luck of the Bodkins*

19. 'Between the courses he danced like something dark and slithery from the Argentine.' *Nothing Serious*

20. 'Wilfred Allsop was sitting up, his face pale, his eyes glassy, his hair disordered. He looked like the poet Shelley after a big night out with Lord Byron.' *Galahad at Blandings*

21. 'It has been well said that an author who expects results from a first novel is in a position similar to that of a man who drops a rose petal down the Grand Canyon of Arizona and listens for the echo.' *Cocktail Time*

22. 'You can't go by what a girl says, when she's giving you the devil for making a chump of yourself. It's like Shakespeare. Sounds well but doesn't mean anything.' *Joy in the Morning*

23. 'Hang it!' said Bill to himself in the cab. 'I'll go to America!' The exact words probably which Columbus had used, talking the thing over with his wife.' *Uneasy Money*

24. 'The aunt made a hobby of collecting dry seaweed, which she pressed and pasted into an album. One sometimes thinks that aunts live entirely for pleasure.' *The Clicking of Cuthbert*

YORKSHIRE SLANG

Just as Cockneys have their own slang so the people of Yorkshire have developed words and phrases which are unique to their county. Here are a dozen of the most commonly used Yorkshire slang words – and their meanings:

1. Aye – Yes
2. Bairn – Child
3. Barmpot – Stupid person
4. Bins – Glasses
5. Champion – Very good
6. Chuddy – Chewing gum
7. Kegs – Trousers/underwear
8. Mardy – Moody
9. Nowt – Nothing
10. Splig – Spider
11. Thou – You
12. Twonk – Idiot

APPENDIX

Famous People Who You Thought Were Born in England – but Weren't

1. Duke of Wellington – born in Dublin, Ireland.
2. Florence Nightingale – born in Florence, Italy.
3. Rudyard Kipling – born in Bombay, India.
4. George Orwell – born in Motihari, Bengal.
5. T. E. Lawrence (Lawrence of Arabia) – born in Wales.
6. St George, patron saint of England – probably born in Cappudocia, an area which is now in Turkey.
7. King Henry V – born in Wales.
8. Tommy Cooper – born in Wales
9. Bertrand Russell – born in Wales.
10. Boris Johnson – born in America
11. Oscar Wilde – born in Ireland
12. Bernard Shaw – born in Ireland

And there are many famous People who you thought weren't born in England but were. For example, David Lloyd George, a professional Welshman and former Prime Minister, was born in Manchester and Gustavus Theodore von Holst, the composer was born in Cheltenham.